VOICES OF WAR

VOICES OF WAR

Front Line and
Home Front

Peter H. Liddle

With an Introduction by John Terraine

Leo Cooper

London

—— in association with ——

4
CHANNEL FOUR TELEVISION

TyneTeesTelevision

940.4

First published in 1988 by Leo Cooper Ltd

Leo Cooper is an independent imprint of the
Heinemann Group of Publishers,
Michelin House, 81 Fulham Road, London SW3 6RB

LONDON   MELBOURNE   JOHANNESBURG   AUCKLAND

Designed by Brooke Calverley
Printed and bound at The Bath Press, Avon

CONTENTS

INTRODUCTION

by John Terraine

O N C E A G A I N Peter Liddle has tipped the cornucopia of his now famous 1914–1918 Archive, to spill out further riches – the photographs and the letters which make up this book, which is his tenth based upon that source. There is no doubt about it, for the British the First World War remains, despite all factual or statistical evidence to the contrary, the 'Great War'. Never mind that at least four times as many lives were lost between 1939 and 1945 as in the first war; never mind that the Western Front's hideous scenes of ravaged desolation were later repeated all the way from Brest to Moscow. 1914–1918, and the Western Front above all, continue to represent the ultimate of war experience for very large numbers of British people. It was the war of the 'Pals' Battalions', of 'Kitchener's Mob'.[1] which remains 'Grandfather's War',[1] 'Great Uncle Fred's War',[1] personalized, a piece of family lore, a haunting tragedy. And by thinking of it so, the British made it so; it became their trauma. That is all the more reason to be thankful that Peter Liddle has chosen to spend so many years and so much effort in catching hold of every scrap of evidence that he could find, whether in words or pictures or other mementoes, that bears upon the vast event, the great unhealed internal scar which constitutes the British trauma.

To the uninitiated all war illustrations are alike, as all war ruins are alike and all war cemeteries are alike – repulsive and boring in the same breath. One group of men or women looking into a camera, one row of solemn or cheerful (or blank) faces, of smart or mud-stained uniforms, look much like another until you know. Wiser readers, more concerned and more perceptive, perceive in these inscrutable groups the individuals whose personal qualities made up the human experience of war for better or for worse. As individuals, these soldiers or airmen, sailors and nurses, are all different; as humans on the moving pavement of time, they change as time determines – a 1915 group is *not* the same as a 1917 group, 1914 and 1918 seem to have travelled a world apart. Their settings – the scenery of war behind and around them in the photographs – change also under the spur of time as ruin advances or recedes. And so we search the pictures time and again to try to unravel their secrets, to comprehend the courage, the endurance, the fear, the strain, the unremitting pressures of conditions that we can never share. These pictures from Peter Liddle's collection had never been publicly exposed until he showed them; the impatient glancer may think he has seen them all before, but he has not. They are doubly new – not only never before published, but, also newly exploring the everlasting differences of individuality – that unfailing characteristic which caused General Glubb, recalling the sight of heaps 'of torn and dirty grey or khaki rags' covered with buzzing swarms of bluebottles, to write:

> One cannot see these ragged and putrid bundles of what once were men without thinking of what they were – their cheerfulness, their courage, their idealism, their love for their dear ones at home. Man is such a marvellous, incredible mixture of soul and nerves and intellect, of bravery, heroism and love – it *cannot* be that it all ends in a bundle of rags covered with flies. These parcels of matter seem to me to be proof of immortality. This cannot be the end of so much.[2]

That is exactly it: that is what makes each war picture different – the possibility of another clue to the 'marvellous, incredible mixture'.

Every country that took part in the First World War suffered, to some extent, from trauma. Some – Serbia, Romania, Belgium – faced direct prospects of national extinction and detested foreign occupation. Others endured horrifying losses: thus France called up one fifth of her entire population; her dead numbered 1,385,300 (compared with some 800,000 for Great Britain), 3.5% of the population (compared with Britain's 1.8%), 18% of those mobilized (compared with 13.6%). Germany had over two million dead – but far worse in many German eyes was the inconceivable, unutterable end result: humiliating defeat and the fall of the Empire. Russia was transformed by an even greater cataclysm whose true character is only now, in 1988, being unravelled. The Austro–Hungarian Empire, heir of the Holy Roman Empire and for centuries Europe's traditional centrepiece, had vanished, leaving only a power vacuum – food for trauma indeed. Yet there can be little doubt that, for assorted reasons, Britain's trauma was the deepest of all.

In this collection Peter Liddle shows us the comprehensive progress of Britain's war, from the first extraordinary flush of 1914 enthusiasm to the dour, grim and seemingly endless grind of the trench warfare stalemate and the sudden, scarcely believable victory at the end. Where, in all this, does the special trauma lie? Was it simply the War that caused it – or was it, perhaps, the Peace? and which Peace do we mean? The 'innocent' peace before 1914? Or the corrupted world after 1918? Or was Britain's trauma the product of all three?

The last alternative is, I think, the most likely. When the British cheered the coming of war in August, 1914, and made their unmistakable statement of feeling about their – to our eyes – somewhat unfeeling native land by flocking to the recruiting stations literally by the million (1,186,357 volunteers by the end of 1914 alone), they truly did not know what they were in for; they were 'innocent' indeed. This was to be their first encounter with major war in the industrial age, the age of the mass populations, the mass armies and the mass casualties, and it would be shocking. But we must be clear about our meaning: not shocking in the sense of sudden revelation; this shock was cumulative.

To begin with, the war was not, as the foolish predicted, 'over by Christmas'; on the contrary, it went on – and on, and on. But only the passing of time could prove that. And with the passing of time a second shock developed. The mighty Royal Navy, on which all British power and, indeed, the British Empire itself, depended, did not open the account with a gratifying series of Trafalgars as many expected. Indeed, it rarely saw its rival, the German battle fleet, but met instead a new underwater enemy – the U-boat – which frightened those who understood its menace more than anything since the Dutch Wars. The island status which had been a source of British contentment for nearly ten centuries now changed its aspect; the island was beleaguered, even threatened with starvation. It also came under attack in another manner never seen before: Zeppelins and Gothas flew over British cities and introduced them to the high explosives that continental cities knew only too well. Physical danger, then, food shortages and rationing, the discomforts of intensive mobilization and conscription, and year by year the obstinate elusiveness of peace, these were the elements of the slow trauma which set in when the delusions of a long security behind the naval shield were swept away.

What was happening – easy enough to see now, but only prophesied or perceived by a very few at the time – was the reckoning for having adopted a continental policy, joining the continental system of alliances, without enquiring what the cost might be and without making due preparations for the continental war which could well result. One consequence, which lay at the root of much loss and frustration, was that in this land warfare which she undertook when the Expeditionary Force crossed to France in 1914, Britain found herself not merely enmeshed in a coalition, but a junior partner at that. This was a slow shock, too, as Lloyd George indicates with his pathetic question to his friend Winston Churchill in January, 1915:

> Are we really bound to hand over the ordering of our troops to France as if we were her vassal?[3]

The proper answer, of course, was 'Yes, certainly, as long as we continue to fight on French soil beside a French army enormously larger than ours'. The great misfortune was that the mass and momentum of the German onslaught in August, 1914, had given Germany an initiative which she continued to enjoy for four years; as I have said elsewhere:

> the French had to dance to the German tune, and the British danced at their coat-tails – an activity neither dignified nor rewarding.

When this message sank in, it also formed a large part of the trauma.

The moment of truth came in 1916; by then France, having already suffered over two million casualties (compared with Britain's approximate half million), was exhausted. The time had come for the British Expeditionary Force to assume the chief rôle on the Western Front – the main theatre of war. Now the British

Army had to take up the fight against the main body of the main enemy for the only time in its history, and with brief intermissions it continued to perform this task until the Armistice. But, thanks to political follies, it also continued to hold junior status.

As may be supposed, it was during this period that the overwhelming majority of British losses occurred. It would, in my opinion, have been a miracle requiring supernatural explanation, if the British had *not* had very heavy losses between 1916–1918. The French losses, when the duty of engaging the main body of the main enemy fell upon them between 1914–1916, had been on a fully matching scale; when it came to Russia's turn to do it, between 1941–1945, her losses were frankly appalling. But 1916 (the year of 'the Somme') was when the British learned the real meaning of modern war. This was when whole towns, whole districts, began to pour out the blood of their young men. Now was the time of the terrible telegrams from the War Office, saying that husbands or sons or brothers would never come home again, the time of the endless lists of casualties in the newspapers, to be scanned with dread every day.

We read of the 'shock' of awareness of the cost of the Battle of the Somme. It was only a shock in the broadest sense; in the more exact, historical sense it is better described as a progressive awareness. It was to do with searching the casualty lists *every day*; with watching the Post Office boy on his red bicycle delivering first one telegram down the street, then another and another. For two more years the swelling march continued towards those hasty graves with their rough crosses that Peter Liddle shows us, the orderly green cemeteries that we know today, the hospitals and the convalescent homes – and for many unfortunates the long years of ruined, hopeless life without limbs or without sight in such institutions as the Star and Garter Home. And while all this was going on a picture began to form which was very different from pre-war notions, from the bland official communiqués and the fatuous, cheery war reports in the newspapers. So a sense of having been deceived began to build up, and this, too, I suggest, would in due course become a powerful ingredient in the trauma.

The voices of an articulate Citizen Army ('the people in uniform') now also made themselves heard:

> Evil and the incarnate fiend alone can be masters of this war, and no glimmer of God's hand is seen anywhere.[4]

Thus Paul Nash, the painter, who set down the landscapes of Hell for all time. Not all perceptions, however, were exactly in this vein.

Lord Chandos (Oliver Lyttelton, Grenadier Guards) echoed Nash in a letter in 1917:

> This country stinks of corruption. As far as the eye can reach is that brown and torn sea of desolation and every yard is a grave, some marked with rifles others with crosses, some with white skulls, some with beckoning hands. But everything is dead: the trees, the fields, the corn, the church ... it is all dead and God has utterly forsaken it.[5]

But then the pipe band of the new Irish Guards strikes up a jaunty tune nearby and Lyttelton continues:

> the pipes and the saffron kilts brought us back to life and the warm red blood of youth and laughter, and we walked among the dead and thought only of the spring and its awakening.

Such are the words by which we read the riddles of the young men in the photographs.

To another of them, Sidney Rogerson, the war

> was not all ghastliness. It was a compound of many things; fright and boredom, humour, comradeship, tragedy, weariness, courage and despair. Those who were lucky lived, and every six or nine months saw most of their friends die. Soon, the places were filled and the daily round went on.[6]

The 'daily round'; this, also, is something we learn about in these photographs and letters – the meanings of the verb, to 'stick it'. It is in them, too, that we find the interpretation of that heart-wrenching pride which caused the soldier in Frederic Manning's battalion, coming out of the line on the Somme, to proclaim:

> They can say what they bloody well like, but we're a fuckin' fine mob.

Or, differently expressed, but amounting to the same thing, Charles Carrington's nine valiant words:

> We were not intimidated by the war of attrition.[8]

This, of course, was the spirit which carried the British Army forward to its 'finest hour' in 1918. In that year, on the defensive with its 'backs to the wall', it inflicted two heavy defeats on the largest array of military might yet seen, and then passed to its own final offensive which began on 8 August ('the black day of the German Army') and concluded with the Armistice. Nine separate and unmistakable victories were won by the British Expeditionary Force (including its ten magnificent Dominion divisions) during this 'Hundred Days' Campaign', the most spectacular of them being the breaking of the 'Hindenburg Line' on 29 September. As Marshal Foch wrote:

Never at any time in history has the British Army achieved greater results in attack than in this unbroken offensive.[9]

And that is as true now as when he wrote it in 1919. It is a truth which strongly suggests that when we look for the true seat of the enduring British trauma, we shall not find it on the Western Front. Overwhelming victory is not a trauma symptom, nor is trauma a victory weapon. The trauma of World War I, in truth, was not in the Army at war; it was in the hearts and minds of the people, deluded before the war, deceived during it and betrayed after it. And nothing displays the strength of the trauma more clearly than the determination with which the British people put the wonderful victory of the Citizen Army out of their minds, and forgot it as though it had never been.

John Terraine

[1] These are all titles of books in my possession.

[2] John Glubb: *Into Battle: A Soldier's Diary of the Great War* p. 67; Cassell 1977.

[3] Martin Gilbert, *Winston S. Churchill III* Companion volume i p. 472: Lloyd George (Chancellor of the Exchequer) to Churchill, 29 January.

[4] Paul Nash, letter to his wife, November 1917.

[5] Lord Chandos, *From Peace to War: A Study in Contrast 1857–1918* p. 182; Bodley Head 1968; letter, May 3 1917.

[6] Sidney Rogerson: *Twelve Days* p. xvii; Arthur Barker, 1933.

[7] Frederic Manning: *The Middle Parts of Fortune* p. 6; Peter Davies 1977.

[8] Charles Carrington: *Soldier from the Wars Returning* p. 123; Hutchinson 1965.

[9] Introduction to *Sir Douglas Haig's Despatches* p. xiii; Dent 1919.

AUTHOR'S PREFACE

F O R Y E A R S I have felt drawn by the need to rescue and preserve the threatened evidence of personal experience in the Great War. The result of this commitment has been the building up of comprehensively catalogued collections which document a remarkably wide range of service and civilian experience through original letters, diaries, photographs, scrapbooks, maps, uniforms and other souvenirs. Recollections recorded on paper and on tape support this evidence. These archives have drawn scholars and visitors from all over the world and have been both the principal source of my own books on the First World War and useful for the work of a number of authors on the same subject.

The grave and the dustbin have been my enemies, but I have had an alliance which has ensured considerable success in an unending battle against time – that is the men and women of 1914–18 and their families. The privilege I have been accorded in such support from all corners of Britain, throughout the Commonwealth and from European countries, particularly from France, is embedded in my conscience. From all walks of life people have offered me long-treasured documents and have spoken or written of matters vividly recalled though seldom expressed. Reaching these people provided one challenge; carefully evaluating all the material gathered was another. Progressively I have been given help over this. The good relationship which has obtained with Sunderland Polytechnic, where the archives have grown, has enabled me to welcome local volunteers who assisted in cataloguing papers and a wider fellowship of aid has been built up with geographically distant former students, with men and women keen to have an academically active retirement or people whose feeling for 1914–18 was answered by out-of-office-hours dedication to the subject.

Tyne Tees Television has for nine years shown an interest in the fruit of this research and was able to convince Naomi Sargant, a Senior Commissioning Editor of Channel Four, that she should see for herself what unrevealed riches lay in the archives. As a result of her visit and ensuing discussions, a Features team led by TTV Producer Heather Ging began planning a series on the Great War which would show the personal story of a man's or woman's war as it unfolded, capturing the immediacy of what was for them a stark today and an unknown tomorrow by the use of photographs, letters and diaries, taken or written with no view to publication beyond family or friends. The series offered a thrilling opportunity to share the fascination of what had been rescued of daily preoccupations during a war now seven decades in our past.

This book follows the line taken by the TV series. The illustrations sometimes convey an attractive, sometimes a chilling frisson of closeness to events long past. The feeling is akin to that aroused by the fresh prints of the fox in pristine snow, stimulating excitement at an untouchable, unseen presence.

Many aspects of British experience of the War are covered but there is no attempt to be comprehensive. Concentration is focused upon the soldier in France and his family in Britain. The airman, the sailor and the soldier on more distant fields, though touched on here, will have to await a later volume. The six sections into which the series and the book are divided grew from the creative considerations of the Television team of Heather Ging, Derek Smith and Mark Lavender in discussions held in the archives. The sheer impact of the war, the transformation of civilian into soldier, what Derek called the 'loss of innocence', almost selected itself as a first topic and then, related to this, a further theme, that of the discord between 'image and reality', invited illustration. 'Life in the line' was followed quite naturally by 'man to man' relationships in the defeminised zone of trench activity, behind which lay the possibility of other areas of comradeship, including that among women in uniformed service in France. Inspirational aid to endurance by 'talisman and crucifix' was chosen as a fifth theme and the final topic had to be the concluding climax of the war, its aftermath and personal legacy.

Interwoven into this fabric is a basic thread, even if not always on the surface, of womanhood. Parental concerns, the perspective of children, the face of both the French friend and the German foe were clearly important too in the selection of photographic images and text but so was the technological framework within which the war was fought. Not infrequently what is presented in this book may be thought provokingly at variance with some commonly held ideas about the 1914–18 War, ideas which from archival witness seem ill-founded. It would be no bad thing if *Voices of War* were to encourage the examination of the 20th Century past in a more open-minded way than has often been the case. Present-day perceptions may provoke us to bewilderment, to admiration, perhaps to scorn, at the collective response in 1914 to times and circumstances so different from our own, when the values held were equally different from those which prevail today, but they will scarcely help us to assess that response or those values in their period setting. The first-hand evidence in this book is of men and women responding to the daily demands of the 1914–18 war years cumulatively crowding upon them. Their constraining framework was the inescapable circumstance of war and this may be considered as a lens through which all is distorted, but each generation views its past through a filter which is considered at the time to be one of accumulated wisdom. The only universal truth here is that the filter will be discarded as new 'wisdom' is accumulated.

A high quality image and an interesting subject were the over-riding criteria for the selection of photographs. In the examination of literally thousands of prints, three general points made an impact. The first was that the social significance of the camera in Britain must have been transformed by the exceptional circumstances of Britons being involved in a Great Power war in Europe and far beyond. Photography in 1914 was not confined to the more affluent classes – Kodak Box Brownie and Vest Pocket Kodak cameras were generally and quite cheaply available, but now, from August onwards, in backyards and at front doors, in training camps, on troopships, in Alexandria or in Boulogne, in industrial premises or on the terraces of stately homes transformed into Voluntary Aid Detachment hospitals, the camera shutter was almost self-activated by the emotional turbulence of new, exciting experiences and heart-rending separations. Familiar faces were there in unfamiliar settings, men and women in a new uniformed identity – 'Our Tom as a Soldier in Egypt,' or, as it might be labelled, 'Me and the Sphinx'. Chemist shops, which hitherto had done largely seasonal business developing prints of summer holiday snaps, were kept well-occupied for at least the first eighteen months of the war.

This leads on to the second point which emerged in studying the photograph collections – that the numerical production dramatically diminished towards the end of 1915. This is not wholly explained by the Army's properly stern view of the private camera on active service, because there is also a diminution, though less marked, on the Home Front. Film being in shorter supply may have been a factor, but we are left with the thought of another contributory and entirely reasonable element, that the circumstances of wartime were losing their novelty, were becoming less remarkable, less worthy of record. The reader may see a further development of this phenomenon as he leafs through the pages of the book and that is the paradoxical one of the swiftness with which men accommodated themselves to the abnormality of war. Human resilience in adversity is an ageless phenomenon. It is perhaps only in the comfortable contemplation of things past and outside our personal knowledge that we call it a phenomenon!

The third point about the illustrations is the wide difference in the circumstance, equipment and vision of the photographer as he took his picture. One can see the studied Victorian pose of the family portrait, or the informal group, or the 'tourist' souvenir of a Pyramid dwarfing its visitors. Side by side with the successes of the Vest Pocket Camera – and they sometimes include photographs in action with all its attendant risks to the man operating the camera and to his subject – are well-composed examples of professional glass-plate photography.

The excellent reproduction of the prints which were usually of small size and sometimes indifferently preserved is due to the superb craftsmanship of Stephen G. Bradwel in Tyne Tees stills department and the matching skill of Albert Snell of Whitburn, Sunderland. New life has been given to many fading images. To Kevin Kelly, a friend and invaluable assistant, a major debt is owed in his research on the captioning. Squadron Leader Nobby Clark, helpful in many aspects of my work, was regularly called away from his cataloguing work to give additional and sometimes corrective information on our captions while Maureen Hine sailed along serenely tackling the backlog of archive administration. Carol Gardner prepared the typescript from a scarcely decipherable manuscript, Barbara Peebles and Maureen Hine helping me, as so often, by retyping edited sections.

During the twelve years of my seeking permanent institutional ownership of the collections, many people have offered encouragement. I would like to pay tribute to the authorities at Sunderland Polytechnic for their consistently supportive stance. From almost every quarter there has been goodwill and, where there were obstruction in finding a happy solution or where there were practical problems which required answering, one man, David Dilks, the distinguished Professor of International History at the University of Leeds, refused to be defeated and worked without stint for a positive goal. More recently in the developing saga, Reg Carr, the

Leeds University Librarian, added his endorsement with the commitment of considerable University resources towards the same end, now seen to be within reach at Leeds. As a result and with generous support drawn from various sources including long term 'friends of the Archives', the collections will, by the time this book appears, be in the Brotherton Library of the University of Leeds. It is my hope that the book will lead to more material being sent to the library where I shall be looking after the 1914–18 area of the University's outstanding Twentieth Century holdings.

Having acknowledged my gratitude to Tyne Tees Television, Channel Four and Leo Cooper for faith in my work, I would like to make a dual dedication to this book: to my wife Louise, whose loving support in every way has sustained me through prolonged anxieties which were more corrosive than a heavy workload, I would like to add David Dilks. David's academic judgement of the archives and his personal friendship carried his rescue concept through to success because of a phenomenal singularity of purpose amidst a multiplicity of competing commitments. We may not always deserve the good fortune in personal relationships which can come our way in life, but a step in the right direction is to acknowledge it as I certainly do with regard to Louise and to David and to many people who have assisted me over the past twenty-five years.

July 1988   Peter H. Liddle, F R HIST S

PART ONE

Loss of Innocence.

THE FACT that overwhelming numbers in virtually all sections of the community showed a readiness to accept, even to welcome, the transformation of their lives during the opening months of the Great War should not be thought surprising. Given the heightened tension at the end of a decade of over-heated and, some may consider, ineradicable nationalism, the response to an external threat was predictably almost universal. Every instinct, deeply inbred and further ingrained by school, church and youth organization and by society as a whole, was affronted by the challenge of an upstart rival bullying a small victim, invading the land of Britain's new-found friend and threatening Britain's position in the world. Pre-war Britain had by no means been a state where peace and contentment reigned; there were obvious fractures in society over Ireland, over working and living conditions and over the wider social and political issues of poverty and underprivilege. All this was voluntarily laid aside in the national emergency. That there were some in the United Kingdom who were not happy to see all things reordered in a new spirit of pre-occupation with the external enemy, and that there was a German perspective too, were of little general consequence. What is a good deal more noteworthy is that those factors which shattered the innocence of ignorant enthusiasm – the nature and cost of the fighting and the length of the war – replaced it not with outrage, escapism and widespread pacifist or political subversion, but with a sort of grim resolve to see things through. As education by trench experience and by Home Front anxieties stripped men and women of the unsuitable fripperies of enthusiasm, the substitute donned, a mantle of stoicism, was infinitely more protective.

Britain's unpreparedness for the war in which she had become engaged was but one of the uncomfortable shocks to be assimilated.

Opposite Days of peace. Workers in Water Street, Elswick, Newcastle upon Tyne, leaving Armstrong Whitworth Works, c1913. (*Newcastle upon Tyne City Libraries*)

Overleaf Harvest, 1914, Whitburn Bents farm near Sunderland, County Durham. For these men, as for so many others, it will be the last time they will work together on the land. The man on the left, the donor of this photograph, will soon volunteer. He will serve in France and Italy and will be awarded the Military Medal. (*J. Maw*)

Her Army was wholly inadequate in number and a new nation in
arms had to be forged for warfare on the continent against the
conscript army of a great land power, to say nothing of the nettle-
rash spread of military obligations ranging from China to many
parts of Africa and the Middle East, to Greece, Italy, Persia and
Russia. Another area but dimly envisaged was the development
required of the new air arm of war.

A further shock for the British public was that new weapons at
sea and the way in which the German High Command chose to use
them to a considerable extent neutralized Britain's naval prepon-
derance. It required the waging of a different war from that of the
decisive battle, the Trafalgar at first confidently then savagely but
unavailingly awaited by an eager British newspaper readership.

For the citizens taking on a new identity as soldiers, uniformed
in more senses than one, there were adjustments to make, new
living and training circumstances to which to become accustomed,
the thrill as well as apprehension of shared adventure, travel and
then danger in the actuality of modern war. While bankclerk and
shipyard worker were experiencing in training their new freedom
from the dull routine of their old life, adjusting to the new con-
straints and finding much about which to grumble, women too
found that they had a rôle to play. Pride in family and friends in
khaki could be extended into active or passive disapproval of young
men who were not in uniform. Service to a brother by letters,
parcels and loving concern could also be extended beyond the
family. At first it was the voluntary organizations into which personal commitment to a national cause could be poured. Later,
women entered areas of industry needing labour as a result of the
inevitable drain into the Army or which required wholesale expansion to meet the needs of the war. Throughout the war the significance to the nation and to women themselves of their taking up the
challenge of new opportunities was fundamental.

A war such as this was simply beyond anticipatory perception.
Boer War memories made wholly inadequate comparison. Dervish
and Zulu were the stuff of lantern slide lectures. The wounded of
the Crimean War and the lengthier anxieties of the wars against
revolutionary France were too far distant and in any case would
have led to more than a touch of embarrassment as the then enemies
were now close allies.

This was no time for a lack of identification with the cause, it was
an opportunity to be in the forefront of patriotic feeling. Germans
in Germany were out of reach but Hartmann the butcher and
Guttmayer the tailor were not, their windows were within a stone's

throw and a Dachshund, a suitably small symbol of the hateful Hun, could be kicked.

Much was being changed, was unfamiliar and exciting but, not least, it was simple. When the Germans, who had done atrocious things in Belgium and France, actually shelled Hartlepool, killing babies in so doing, when they sank a 'passenger liner', the *Lusitania*, tried and shot a British woman, Edith Cavell, by military tribunal, and actually dropped bombs on the capital city of the British Empire, it was abundantly clear that Germans were wicked beyond redemption – except through the lesson of a complete and utter defeat. Such a defeat could only be achieved by everyone doing his bit. Of course such attitudes and such actions increasingly needed organizing into a National will to win. Everything and everybody would be subject in some degree to the Nation's need. New opinions and new attitudes would be shaped, as well as the reaffirmation of some old prejudices, but what would finally emerge from the crucible of war, how long the struggle would last and whether it were likely to be proved worthwhile, these were questions which exercised the minds of that smaller percentage of people not totally preoccupied with their daily concerns of trench, hospital, factory or kitchen. They, as Asquith enjoined, would just have to "wait and see".

Seaside idyll, June, 1914 at Seaford in Sussex. Captain Oliver Hogg, Royal Field Artillery, took this photograph of his wife and daughter Maureen. On 26 August he was to leave Southampton in command of one of the first two anti-aircraft detachments of the British Expeditionary Force. (*Brigadier O. F. G. Hogg*)

Summer, 1914, before the outbreak of war. Bank clerks from the private bank of Cocks and Biddulph in Whitehall. Jack Bentham, on the extreme right, and perhaps the youngest at 23, is on the threshold of a most unusual war service – a Royal Naval Volunteer Reserve Able Seaman with the Royal Naval Brigade at Antwerp in October, 1914, internment in and escape from Holland, Gallipoli in 1915 and then Commissioned Service on the Western Front still with the Royal Naval Division, in 1916. Finally, as a Royal Naval Air Service flying-boat pilot, on anti-submarine patrols in 1918. (*J. H. Bentham*)

Just prior to the outbreak of war and men of B Company of the 4th Battalion, King's Royal Rifles, are awaiting warning of an attack, during manoeuvres in the Chitta Hills, near Mackam in India. The Battalion would soon be en route for Europe to serve under very different conditions. (*General Sir Evelyn Barker, a 1914 Subaltern in the King's Royal Rifles*)

Summer camp at Buddon, Carnoustie, near Dundee, in 1914. Some moments of rest for an officer of the 1st Northumbrian Royal Field Artillery Brigade, Territorial Force. (*Major H. Pybus of this Brigade*)

August, 1914, and the Red Cross Working
Party at Burton Constable in Yorkshire is
photographed exemplifying an early stage of
readiness from which an enormous
expansion of women's voluntary service was
to be realized. (*Miss P. Baldwin*)

A detachment of First Aid Nursing Yeomanry lined up for inspection. Founded in 1907, this women's uniformed volunteer corps prepared itself thoroughly in peacetime to serve its country in the event of war. The photograph is taken in the summer of 1913 and, within a year, women of the corps will have crossed the Channel to serve in the war, but ironically to serve Belgian soldiers as the British War Office showed initial reluctance to employ them. (*Miss B. Hutchinson, a member of the Corps at that time*)

Overleaf Territorials of the Black Watch cross the River Tay by ferry on 4 August, 1914, to their war station at Tayport in Fife, Scotland. *L to R*, Privates Cosgrove, Moore, Chadwick, Calvert and Edwards, the donor of the photograph. (*Rev T. W. Edwards*)

Barcombe in Sussex and the encamped 1st Staines Troop of the Middlesex Boy Scouts salute the flag at the outbreak of war. (*Brigadier C. Greenslade, one of the troop's Scoutmasters in 1914*)

Aldershot: Three Regular Army Royal Engineer despatch riders. *L to R*, Corporals Perks, Daish and Hodder are ready to depart for France with the 1st Division, British Expeditionary Force, which began leaving Southampton within a week of the declaration of war. (*J. N. R. Perks*)

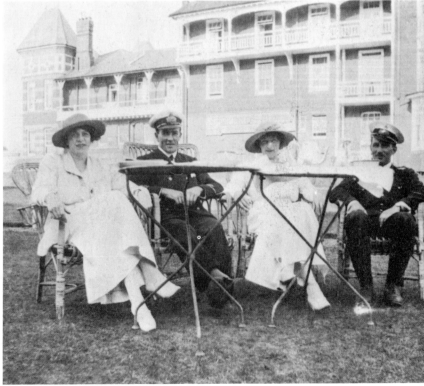

Right Westgate-on-Sea: St Mildred's Hotel and its grounds are already in August, 1914, accommodating an RNAS Advanced Seaplane Station. An enclosure normally used to store bathing machines was particularly convenient for the seaplanes as it included a slipway to the beach. Pictured here from the left are Miss Morten, Sub-Lieutenant Fowler RN, Mrs Downs and Lieutenant Kilner RMLI. Kilner went out to the Dardanelles with HMS *Ark Royal* as a seaplane pilot, as did the donor of this photograph whose diary entry during the critical days at the outbreak of the war included his thanks to God that "I've had the luck to be alive and in the Navy on 'The Day'". (*Air Vice-Marshal Sir Geoffrey Bromet*)

A seaplane version of the Henry Farman
F20. This particular aircraft was delivered
to the Royal Naval Air Service in August,
1914, and is seen taxiing to its home station
of Calshot on the Solent. (*Air Vice-Marshal
Sir Geoffrey Bromet*)

The Lord Mayor of Bristol leads a recruiting rally through the city streets in the early days of the war. (*Madge Angus*)

The Grahame-White XV was an aircraft of pre-war design belonging to the 'Boxkite' period, but it found wartime use as a trainer for beginners. Leslie Horridge is the pupil in the pilot's seat. He is at the Grahame White School at Hendon and upon his acceptance into the Royal Flying Corps will be refunded the £75 cost of his schooling. (*Wing Commander G. H. Lewis*)

3 September, 1914, Chelmsford. The 4th
Battalion Royal Berkshire Regiment
(Territorial Force) has been billeted in the
city since 24 August, but as the men march
through the streets they still bring shopping
and business momentarily to a standstill.
The battalion remained here until it
entrained for France on 30 March, 1915.
(*Dr G. Moore, 4th Bn Royal Berks*)

September, 1914, Sefton Park, Liverpool
and the 'Liverpool Pals', volunteers for the
King's Liverpool Regiment, line up for
their Army pay. The men are still in their
civilian clothes and the donor of the
photograph has marked his position with an
arrow. It must have been a strange and
exciting sight for the little girl on the left
with her hoop. (*F. Hindle*)

Goodbye, New Zealand. The scene at the quayside, Wellington, New Zealand, as the troopship SS *Devon* leaves with over nine hundred reinforcements for the 1915 Dardanelles campaign. This troop transport made several such voyages under the command of Captain H. W. Robertson, Mercantile Marine. (*Dame Anna Neagle, Captain Robertson's daughter*)

Canadian farewells. In the late summer of
1914 the troopship *Princess Sophia* leaves a
Canadian landing stage. Poignant scenes
such as this of soldiers leaving their families
for a distant war and an uncertain future
were taking place throughout the Empire.
Some of the troops here are wearing pith
helmets and some, like the extroverts in the
rigging, are kilted. (*Colonel E. A. P. Hobday*)

An intriguing mixture of stern resignation
and whimsical humour shown by Mess
Orderlies of the 'Liverpool Pals' in their
Mess Hall at Prescot, Liverpool in
November, 1914. (*A. Tongue, King's
Liverpool Regiment*)

Exactly a year after the outbreak of war, one of Kitchener's New Army Divisions, the 61st, is ready for the Field-Marshal's personal inspection at Highlands Park near Chelmsford. One of the men inspected by the Field-Marshal and the donor of this photograph, wrote to his friend on 14.8.15, "We had to be really polished up for this occasion and, as we were quite close to the great man, I actually heard him say a few kind words". (*L. B. Stanley, RAMC*)

The band of a Scottish regiment training in Essex attracts the people of Coggeshall and entertains men from other units billeted in this small town near Colchester. (*H. H. Frost, 21st London Regiment*)

Men of the 7th Battalion, Durham Light Infantry at their camp in Heworth, Gateshead in 1915. Though serving in a Territorial battalion, William Allan, third from the left in the back row, wears his Imperial Service Obligation Badge indicating that he had volunteered for overseas service at the outbreak of war. He was under age and therefore spent further months in training. Next to Allan is a coloured soldier, a rare phenomenon in an United Kingdom unit during the First World War. Most of the men have the old-pattern leather equipment but some have the new-style webbing. (*W. Allan*)

Ashford in Kent early in 1915 and three men of the 7th Battalion, Durham Light Infantry, are photographed outside the home of the family upon whom they are billeted. (*W. Maughan of 7th DLI*)

Right Soldiers in Sheffield. The original caption to go with this photograph taken in a family backyard, "Bumming teas on a Sunday", makes no bones about the purpose of the visit. (*P. H. L. Archives*)

Opposite The stern eye of Sergeant Cobley ensures that men of C Company, 12th Battalion, Northumberland Fusiliers combine correct technique with due ferocity in Chiltern Hills bayonet training (1915). (*Air Chief Marshal Sir Roderic Hill, at that time a subaltern in this battalion*)

Rifleman Ronald Morton of the London
Rifle Brigade entering his shared billet at
Haywards Heath in the winter of 1914–15.
(*R. C. Morton*)

A route march on a hot day for the 'Liverpool Pals' (the 17th Battalion, The King's Liverpool Regiment). (*E. W. Willmer, 17th Battalion, King's Liverpool Regiment*)

Lieutenant John Gardner, an instructor at
the Machine Gun Corps School, Belton
Park, Grantham, demonstrates his art on the
firing range (1918). Note that the
ammunition belt is blurred – the Vickers
machine-gun had a firing rate of 600 rounds
per minute. (*J. G. H. Gardner*)

Assessing the marksmanship of Territorials of the Devonshire Regiment on the Hyde Heath firing range of Wareham, Dorset in October, 1916. (*R. C. Morton, at this date a subaltern in the 9th Duke of Cornwall's Light Infantry*)

Scottish Territorials in training, Devon, spring, 1915. In white, the 14th Battalion, Argyll and Sutherland Highlanders, rise above their opposition in this unit football match near Ashburton. (*J. D. Mackie, 14th Bn, Argyll and Sutherland Highlanders*)

Below Late February, 1915, and a very early breakfast – 3 a.m. – on an important day for the 5th Battalion, South Staffordshire Regiment. They are to be inspected by His Majesty the King and then to embark for overseas service. (*F. Wilkinson of this Battalion*)

Bound for France: Men of the 5th Battalion, South Staffordshire Regiment cross the Channel aboard the Isle of Man Steam Packet Company vessel *Empress Queen*. For many it would be for the first time and for some, of course, the last. (*F. Wilkinson*)

An aspect of (and from) the 'New Dimension' of warfare. The Royal Flying Corps aerodrome at Waddington near Lincoln in December, 1917, when it housed three training squadrons. In spite of the snow, flying is still in progress with numerous aeroplanes in evidence on the right of the photograph. It is probable that the SS airship is from the Royal Naval Air Service Station at Cranwell ten miles to the South of Waddington. (*T. H. Newsome, RFC*)

Buenos Aires in May, 1917, and the Cruiser HMS *Glasgow* fires a salute on entering this great port of neutral Argentina. HMS *Glasgow* spent much of her war service in South American waters and was present at the December, 1914 Battle of the Falkland Islands. (*Rear Admiral B. Sebastian, then an officer in HMS* Glasgow)

A picture for which innumerable soldiers posed. Here the tall figure on the left is Quartermaster Sergeant Stanley Rous of the Royal Field Artillery. His 'Egyptian' diary records frequent refereeing of football matches, the dirty play of the Army Pay Corps and the presence of a certain "Major Lawrence" at one game. (*Sir Stanley Rous*)

An old French mill frames the scene of a
roadside halt for British troops and the
low-flying BE2c beyond.
(*A. H. Gitsham, RFC*)

"C" Coy. 5ᵀᴴ Connaught
Rangers,
On the Road To Le Cateau.
5·40 P.M. 10/10/18.
A.M.P.

Issue biscuits and trench life were not exclusively responsible for Army dental problems; the state of the Nation's teeth in 1914 was far from pearly white. Here in April, 1918, in the main laboratory of the Army Dental Clinic, Harfleur, near Le Havre, dental mechanics are busy using blow lamps to melt wax as they cast moulds for dentures. The donor of this photograph is arrowed "J.D.C.". (*J. D. Creighton, RAMC*)

Opposite A shell bursts among men of the 5th Connaught Rangers as they are about to storm Le Cateau on 10 October, 1918. Immediately behind the unfortunate soldiers depicted here waited 2nd Lieutenant McPeake with his supporting section. Before long McPeake was himself wounded and, as he convalesced, within weeks of the drama at Le Cateau, he painted this scene from memory. (*A. Y. McPeake*)

Bombardment of Hartlepools, Dec. 16th, 1914.
Belk Street.

The damage to housing in Hartlepool on the morning of 16 December, 1914, when three German battlecruisers shelled this North-Eastern port. 119 men, women and children were killed in the town and Scarborough and Whitby were also shelled. The British public was outraged, but not all the outrage was directed towards the Germans. Had not the Royal Navy failed to protect British shores? If Hartlepool suffered, recruitment to the services discernibly benefited. (*S. Winkcup*)

Overleaf A ten-year-old girl writes to her 'Grannie' of a Gotha bomber raid on London in the summer of 1917. In this raid twenty-two Gothas attacked. Civilian casualties were fifty-seven killed and 193 injured. (*Brigadier W. M. T. Magan*)

This confectionery van has come off the worse for wear in an August, 1916, collision at Crooksbury Hill near Farnham in Surrey. It was hit by a VAD ambulance bearing convalescent wounded soldiers, two of whom pose, having survived the accident without further injury. (*Mrs May Dunlop, at this time a VAD nurse at Waverley Abbey as Miss May Justice*)

25 Alexander
St W2
July 8th 1917

My dear Grannyie.
    I hope you are all well.
On saterday we were just
lookning for some chepe
pealoer when we saw 20
    German earplains up
    over our heds and the
english were shouting at
them and they flew right
over our house and we
could see all the pufs
of smoke and now and then
one of them would be
coverd with smoke and
then come out again

quite safe and all the
trafake were flyning
aklonge and all the
pople standning out on
the street and every
boddy stoped buying
and ran out in the
street and the streets
was full of pople,
But the earplains did
not do any damage here
but they did a lot of
damage in the sity
37 pople killed and 137
wonded, and they droped
a bom on Gamages and
I have not heard yet how
many Pople were killed.
With best love from
Sheelah Magan

Return to France after Home Leave. Rifleman Ronald Morton and his family at Victoria Station on 29 June, 1915. His father has his back to the camera, mother is just visible over father's left shoulder. (*R. C. Morton, 1st London Rifle Brigade*)

This 12-inch rail-mounted big gun at
Armstrong Whitworth's Elswick Works,
Newcastle upon Tyne in 1916, appears
ready for delivery. Despite its mounting,
one may imagine that its eventual arrival at a
railhead siding for action would not be
without delays and problems en route.
(*Vickers plc*)

Left This photograph taken in 1915
shows the five Thorburn brothers. Four
are clearly officers in Scottish regiments;
the fifth, Jim, in civilian clothes, is
strictly speaking not at war with anyone as
he had become a citizen of the then
neutral United States of America where
he had been living, representing the
family textile firm. (*Colonel M. M.
Thorburn, 2nd Bn, Black Watch*)

Right A postwar studio portrait of the
Stoneham family with its varied record of
service in the Great War. On the left is
Captain Hugh Stoneham OBE, a pre-war
Regular Army Officer in the East Surrey
Regiment. In the centre is Flight Lieutenant
Gerald Stoneham RAF, who had served
earlier in the Infantry. On the right is
Captain Cecil Stoneham, Royal Engineers.
The brothers are pictured with their sister
Olive, a member of a Red Cross Voluntary
Aid Detachment.
(*Squadron Leader G. T. Stoneham*)

PART TWO

Image and Reality.

I N BEING struck, as we cannot fail to be, by the gulf between the reality of the fighting in France and the image of that fighting as presented in Britain, we should remind ourselves of two considerations. The incapacity to perceive with any degree of accuracy sights or scenes wholly outside one's own experience is universal. We may say of a previously unvisited holiday resort that it was just as we pictured it, but we will have had brochures, guides and TV pictures to build our own image and there will have been no unanticipated human activity on the scene. Secondly, and with specific relation to the image of trench warfare in 1915–17, it was entirely reasonable and necessary that there should be such a gap between imagination of the rôle of the soldier at the front and the actual lot of men in the line. The morale of no section of the United Kingdom community would be aided by constant pictorial or verbal truth about battle, about being under heavy shelling or facing a trench raid. If one were to judge that the soldier in training might have been better prepared for the shock of his introduction into the line, we may remind ourselves of the splendid 1944 story related by Kenneth Macksey of the psychologically ill-judged decision to show men of the Royal Tank Corps a captured Tiger tank that they might familiarise themselves with their principal armoured opponent once they had landed in Normandy. "We were terrified," was Macksey's frank admission. Mothers, wives, sisters, fathers, would certainly not go about their daily business uplifted by chilling testimony of what a loved one was facing and when that daily business was the vital one of building ships, manufacturing shells, raising produce, running a household or a whole range of essential Home Front employment, we can see that gulf there had to be. Music Hall songs, cinema shows, newspaper headlines, public announcements were quite properly harnessed to the war effort and

Opposite Idyllic interlude. A British officer on detachment with a French unit is taken fishing on the River Oise in July, 1916. (*William Aitchison, R.F.A.*)

not self-injuriously restricted to factually based material.

With regard to Army Censorship against the careless concession of any military Intelligence to the enemy, the soldier himself would usually support rather than undermine morale at home by voluntarily excluding from his letter details which would further raise apprehension. This lack of graphic communication by letter to convey the reality of life in the trenches was not compensated by fireside talks on leave, because, added to reluctance even then to say more, was an incapacity to describe something which the soldier felt lay outside the comprehension of his family or sweetheart. Hence the gulf between image and reality was accepted and acknowledged by those who knew the reality. Naturally this did not drain the resentment they felt at the information purveyed in some newspaper accounts or at the pompous pronouncements of some public figures as they strove to raise to fever heat their audience's emotional commitment to the war. Well aware of the Army censorship of his own letters, the soldier reserved his ridicule or vented his spleen upon war reporting when it was flagrantly at variance with his own experience. It was difficult for him to appreciate that the *Daily Mail's* self-portrayal as helping to win the war had a measure of truth in it.

Some false images would actually be tested in war, be exposed in their misconception, but would not totally be expunged for a variety of reasons. The anticipated active rôle of Cavalry is a particularly good example of this. It remains difficult to explain, even in terms of the expectation of a short war won by swift movement, how there could have been so much faith in the mounted arm when opposed by the quick-firing field gun, the machine gun and the magazine rifle firing from concealed defensive positions. Years and years of training to acquire professional competence in mounted action with sword or lance were brought to swift unproductive conclusion by fire from behind an obstruction or a loop-holed farm building in the very first days of action.

Some images – the football to be kicked across No Man's Land in battle attack, the skirl of the pipes to inspire that same terrible crossing – achieved a degree of immortality. Such sporting concepts or national traditions would challenge modern technological warfare but would either be rudely demolished or would require wholesale modification to meet the circumstance of warfare in 1915.

It should be remembered that the footballs and the bagpipers did, however, have a continuing part to play – on the Home Front. Quite as important a weapon as a gun for the waging of a war involving the whole population were the agencies to boost morale at home. Propaganda, for obvious reasons with regard to National Socialism, Fascism and Communism in the inter-war period, has in public perception today a wholly discredited reputation. This is a singularly one-eyed view of an absolutely essential weapon of war. Some of its most successful proponents have rightly been exposed as disreputable windbags in themselves and it is very easy in present day peacetime contemplation to pour scorn on numerous aspects of Government-inspired propaganda during the First World War. It is also hard scientifically to evaluate the effectiveness of propaganda in separately identifiable campaigns or as a whole. What can be said is that the 'Domestic Front War', whether it were to economise against food shortages or produce more ships or guns, could not be lost or the war would have been lost – and, in the end, the war was won.

The very image which is most likely to affront us in our times, that of glory being won out of war, had in 1916 a direct utility in the war effort. Today we are likely to see the utility of the concept of a glorious sacrifice as being at best a peculiar inversion of Christ's

The lure of Army pageantry: Bandsmen of the Grenadier Guards, inspiration to soldier and civilian alike. (*P. H. L. Archives*)

selflessness but there is no doubt that there was solace for many at home in the wide recognition that to have served and died for one's country was indeed a glorious sacrifice which had a kinship to that of Christ's suffering on the Cross. There is abundant evidence that this image did bring comfort, though we know too that for some there was no easing of their sorrow.

It might well be added here that if any subject were to need an alternative image from that of reality, it would be a soldier's death or serious wounding. It is surely beyond the limit of all but the most stoic to cope with a vision of a son dismembered into unrecognisable fragments by shell explosion – hence the official communication formula 'killed in action' was, in that sense, a consoling kindness.

There is nice irony in the fact that the savage Home Front picture of the 'Hun' was by no means necessarily shared by the men in khaki. This has a further parallel in that the soldier frequently had a less than idealised picture of the French and Belgian peasants whose land he was helping to protect, or of the French and Belgian soldiers, always portrayed at home of course as our suffering friends and gallant allies.

In such a world of contrasts, separations, stress, fear, hope and uncertainty, a world of almost alternative realities, rumour lodged itself quite naturally. The most persistent and beneficent rumour sustained the spirit of the credulous and provided, even at the time, a source of amusement to the sceptic. Occasionally rumour leapt the Channel and did so more effectively than other images could make that crossing, narrow in The First World War only in its miles.

Bruce Bairnsfather's artistic image attempts to bridge the gap between the soldier's active service world and the wife awaiting him at home.

"How long have you got Fred?"

"LEAVE"

What better for a target in a sporting event than the image of Kaiser Wilhelm, the subject of much scorn and bitterness in British public opinion. Here Colonel Hobday is aiming at the Kaiser in a Royal Field Artillery Sports Day at Folkestone in 1915. (*Colonel E. A. P. Hobday*)

Opposite The British, Australian and New Zealand mounted regiments assembled in Egypt would have to leave their horses behind when they served in the 1915 Gallipoli Campaign. The Egyptian Campaign in the Western Desert and then Eastwards towards Gaza and into Palestine would, however, see the horse in action as well as conveying its trooper over a great many miles of harsh terrain. Here the 4th Waikato Squadron of the Auckland Mounted Rifles, New Zealand Expeditionary Force, ride past Shepheard's Hotel in Cairo on 23 December, 1914, during an Imperial show of strength to quell any pro-Turkish or anti-British sentiment. (*J. Palmer, Auckland Mounted Rifles*)

A considerable trial for cavalry was that of the South African 1st Mounted Brigade on its long, demanding trek across a volcanic desert terrain and bare scrubland to Kondoro in 1916 in an attempt to sever German communications in the East African campaign. Here the Brigade is photographed en route, with the South African General van Deventer, the middle figure of the three horsemen on the right. (*Air Chief Marshal Sir Hugh Saunders, at that time in the Witwatersrand Rifles, Union of South Africa Force*)

Many British passenger liners were redeployed to act as troopships and hospital ships. In this case the new troopship on its way to Egypt seems to have retained some of its pre-war trappings. (*Brig. J. A. C. Taylor*)

A poster issued by the Parliamentary Recruiting Committee which still relies upon the image of the charging cavalryman for its impact, despite knowledge that the actual conditions in France did not allow for such dashing gallantry. (*P. H. L. Archives*)

From Private to General

They all enjoy a wash with

WRIGHT'S
Coal Tar Soap

(The Soldiers' Soap.)

It Soothes, Protects, Heals.

In United Kingdom, 4d. per Tablet.

In Australia, Canada, India, and British Colonies, 6d. per Tablet.

Oh for a Cake of "Pears" now!

FOR THE BOYS AT THE FRONT

Just put a cake of

Pears' Soap

in the next parcel of presents you are sending.   It greatly

Enhances the Joy of the Wash and the Shave

Large cakes supplied in 3 tablet boxes convenient for enclosing in parcel; it takes up very little room.

Printed by EYRE & SPOTTISWOODE, LTD., His Majesty's Printers, at East Harding Street, London, E.C., and Published by ... AND TATLER, LTD., Great New Street, London, E.C. May 29, 1915.
Entered as Second-class Matter at the New ...

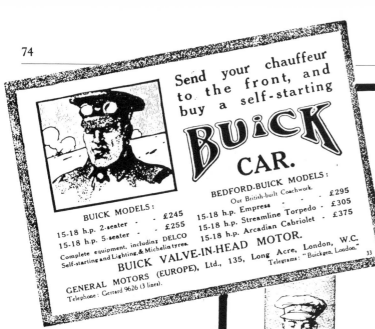
This and previous two pages Commercial advertising was an attractively equalizing image to capture the lucrative market of civilians purchasing toiletries to send off to their menfolk overseas. (*from* The Sphere)

Opposite top Part of the process of turning civilians into useful soldiers was that of 'licking them into shape'. This was the responsibility of Army Physical Training Instructors who were themselves brought up to scratch in the Army Gymnasium at Aldershot. Would-be PTIs are shown assuming a variety of postures for the camera. (*T. E. Stirk, a would-be PTI*)

Opposite below "Joe" – perhaps inaptly named but certainly an appropriate breed for a Naval mascot on board the new 15-inch-gun Dreadnought battleship HMS *Queen Elizabeth*. (*Admiral Sir T. H. Binney, then an officer in HMS* Queen Elizabeth)

The Royal Navy. His Majesty King George
V aboard HMS _Queen Elizabeth_, in this final
year of the war, flagship of the Grand Fleet.
(_H. M. Burrows, HMS_ Benbow)

Definitely not Queensberry Rules. Close-order fighting instruction for the 12th Battalion, Northumberland Fusiliers, in spring, 1915, at their training camp in the Chilterns. (*Air Chief Marshal Sir Roderic Hill, at that time a Subaltern in the Regiment*)

Image amidst reality. A Sergeant-Major in the Royal Engineers uses a souvenir of the March 1915 Battle of Neuve Chapelle to strike a pose for the camera in imitation of the Kaiser. (*W. O. Ridley, RE*)

German soldiers gathered in full battle
order in an underground shelter. From
their expressions it is possible that the
trench system above is under Allied bombardment
preparatory to an infantry attack which the
men here will have to stem when the barrage
lifts. (*C. G. T. Dean, RGA*)

A mixed column of French and Scottish troops being marched to the rear by a German escort. The civilians of an occupied town look on, the impact upon their morale being all too readily imagined. (*T. H. Newsome, ASC and RAF*)

Horatio Bottomley adds his weight to the
recruiting campaign for the London
Regiment (Royal Fusiliers), Trafalgar
Square, August, 1915.
(from *Radio Times Hulton Picture Library*)

Nellie Taylor, a Musical Comedy artiste
with a visiting Concert Party at Ludgershall
camp in Hampshire, adds her charm to the
firing point of a rifle range and helps to make
a persuasive recruiting photograph.
(*J. G. H. Gardner, 5th Essex Regiment*)

Above August, 1917, and John Cooper enjoys the sands at Blyth while his father, Lt-Commander V. M. Cooper, from his submarine base in this Northumberland port, serves in undersea protection of coastal shipping. (*V. M. Cooper*)

Under age and under fire, Private H. I. Rochford, (5th Battalion, South Staffordshire Regiment) who landed in France when still aged 15 and was wounded in May, 1915, just after his sixteenth birthday. He was Orderly to the donor of this photograph. (*F. Wilkinson*)

Opposite Postcard humour of differing degree and directed at different targets keeps spirits up and resolve resolute. (*P. H. L. Archives*)

For gootness sake go back ! Here kom der SURREYS

WELL DONE BELGIUM !

"OH LORD TAKE CARE OF KITCHENER FOR IF ANYTHING SHOULD HAPPEN TO HIM, WE'D HAVE NOBODY TO LOOK AFTER US BUT THE DAILY MAIL."

The Blandford Express.

ADVERTISEMENT COLUMN.

PRELIMINARY NOTICE.

Messrs. WILHELM, SONS & Co.,
BUTCHERS and LOOTERS,
Potsdam, Germany,
(Branch Offices: VIENNA and CONSTANTINOPLE)

Beg to announce that they intend shortly to
OPEN new Branch Establishments in

☞ **London, Paris and Petrograd.** ☜

Further Particulars will be duly announced.

TREATIES SCRAPPED ON THE SHORTEST NOTICE

MURDERS and OUTRAGES
Executed with the Greatest Dispatch.

BOMBS FOR THE BABIES
Free by Zeppelin's Express Delivery.

Buildings Demolished
WHILE YOU WAIT.
(CATHEDRALS A SPECIALITY).

A Few Unsolicited Testimonials
as to our thoroughness and efficiency.

KING ALBERT writes : "The Result of your efforts in
Belgium is simply amazing . . . You have done
your work only too well"
THE ARCHBISHOP of RHEIMS writes : "One can
hardly recognize the Cathedral since your last visit."
THE MAYOR of HARTLEPOOL says : "I am con-
vinced that your men are PERFECT LADY-
KILLERS (also Children)."
ADMIRAL JELLICOE wires : "We look forward with
eagerness to your next visit."
SIR JOHN FRENCH writes : "I will place my orders
shortly when I reach Berlin."
PRESIDENT WILSON cables : I cannot express my
appreciation of your humane methods"

TELEGRAMS :   TELEPHONE : (read upsidedown).
"KULTUR, BERLIN."   773H   J.F.W.

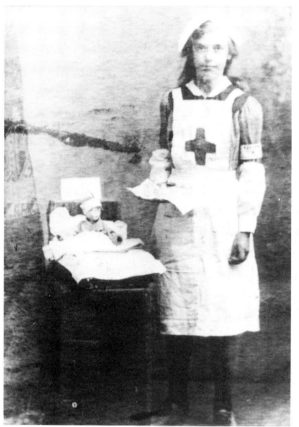

Elizabeth and John Beviss at Wambrook near Chard, in Somerset, both too young to do more than 'identify' in 'doing their bit' in 1914–18 but both to serve their country a generation later. (*Mrs Dora Scott*)

A Somerset girl and her unknown soldier's
morale. Farmer's daughter Ethel Lawrence
of High Church Farm, Hemington, Bath
'did her bit' in knitting socks as her gift for
the Somerset Light Infantry. Her note with
the socks wished the soldiers who got them
good luck and added; "I should like to hear
from you. If there is anything you would like
and can't get it if you will let me know I will
do my best for you." The recipient, Percy
Maggs, asked for and received this
photograph of Ethel in November, 1916.
(*P. Maggs*)

Over the Top

Military Two-Step.

Dance Invented by

James Finnigan.

Music by

Gordon Mackenzie.

No 1216. *Lawrence* **6D** *Wright's* Edition.

GREAT GUNS

Grand Selection of Popular Song Successes

WITH WORDS & TONIC SOL-FA.

Arranged by **Lawrence Wright.**

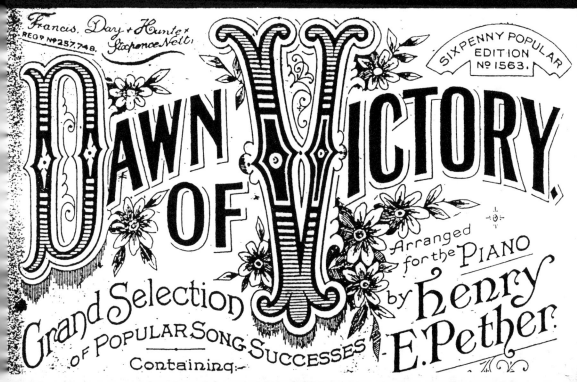

Francis, Day + Hunter
REGD Nº 257.748. Sixpence Nett.

SIXPENNY POPULAR EDITION Nº 1563.

DAWN OF VICTORY.

Grand Selection of Popular Song Successes Containing

Arranged for the PIANO *by* **Henry E. Pether.**

Flies swarm over the boards enclosing a meat stall in Palestine, highlighting the problem of containing sources of infection in hot climates. (*D. B. Watson, 2/10 Middlesex Regiment*)

Actuality from the air. When the public was informed through the Press that gains had been made in late September, 1917, during the 3rd Battle of Ypres, they would not have been able to envisage the devastation around Zonnebeke Church and lake as shown in these military photographs taken by No 21 Squadron RFC, the vertical one taken on 28 September and the oblique one four days later. (*C.E. Townley, Suffolk Regiment, attached RFC*)

This photograph taken in August, 1914, of
Private Wilson of the South Staffordshire
Regiment was published in the Roll of
Honour of his local paper on receipt of the
report that he was missing, believed killed in
action, at Suvla Bay, Gallipoli on 5
September, 1915. He had in fact only been
wounded. (*A. Wilson*)

Remnants: Eighteen Signallers remain on 1 July, 1917, of the fifty-three signallers of the 21st Service Battalion, King's Royal Rifles, who landed in France fourteen months earlier. We must not assume that all the thirty-five missing men had become casualties but the percentage of transfers and promotion would have been small. (*G. V. Dennis, 21st (S) Battalion, KRRC*)

Tea on the beach, Malta, June, 1916, for a recovered patient and two of the nurses from St Andrew's Hospital, Sisters Enright and Kane. The soldier, Teddy Pearson, an officer, was on the point of returning to active service. He was killed a few weeks later on 2 August. (*Sister Kane, QAINS, at St Andrew's Hospital, Malta*)

8.

find Lieut. Co. C.F.'s & settle to occupy
tent with him.   Get settled & learn the
Geography of the Camp.
          Guns busy - Roads packed with
troops & traffic.

②

July 31.   The Great Offensive starts at 4.0 a.m.
Awakened by the deafening Roar of the guns
which in spite of being very lively all night
worked up to "forte" by 4.0 & kept it up all
day till by 9.0 p.m. it had reached "fortissimo"
Such a din you never heard.
One cannot help saying of the poor wounded
"Thank God they are at least spared this".
      One of the hardest days I have ever spent.
Rise 3.45 H.C. 4.15. — Walking wounded
began to come in in crowds at 8.0.
      Helped to marshal them & to write cards &
be generally useful with them till 12.30.
      The heat & the crush in the marquees was
terrific —   Rested 12.30 – 1.
      After lunch on duty with Serious wounded.
— did not find many as they were passing

'Rise 3.45, Holy Communion 4.15, walking wounded begin to come in in crowds at 8.0.' A Padre's diary from a Casualty Clearing Station on the opening day of the 3rd Battle of Ypres, 31.7.17. (*Rev. M. L. Couchman, the Padre*)

through remarkable fast. — Turned on to try
& speed up & generally organize the walking
wounded — managed to get some kind
of order out of the muddle — Busy then
till 8.30. Supper & bed.

    The cheerfulness — Gratitude — Patience
of the wounded is simply beyond description
    The wounds something indescribable
No one can realize what a Hell on earth
modern intensive warfare is that has not
seen the wreckage of humanity that came
back.

    Aug 1. Raining hard all the night & all day
two — Ground simply soaking — Rapidly turning
to a glorious mud swamp:—
    Very bad for the Advance — In fact it is temporarily
"off" — Guns almost silent — Wounded
coming through very slowly all day — simply
soaked through — & plastered with mud & chilled
to the marrow.
    On duty at odd times all day — all other
G/E except Haw & I sent back to their units

Smiles for the camera above a pitiable case at St Andrew's Hospital, Malta. The patient, Gunner Baldwin, has lost his legs and his arms. (*Sister Kane. QAINS Sister at this hospital*)

No 3 Ward of No 2 British Red Cross Hospital at Rouen. In the angled bed is a badly burned airman. (*Mrs I. Smythe, at that time a VAD Nurse in this hospital as Miss Maxtone Graham*)

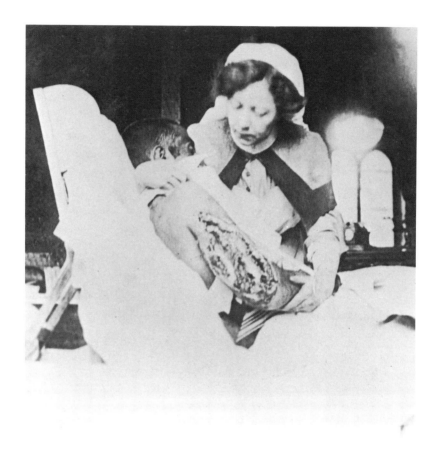

Closer evidence of the reality of what is
likely to have been a shell fragment wound.
(*L. W. Jacques, RAMC*)

PART THREE

Life in the Line.

THE EXPRESSION 'in the line' meant something unequivocal to the First World War soldier. A soldier in the line was not just in France, he was not in a Base Camp or a billet or marching up to the front. He was near the line when he was in reserve trenches, nearer still in support positions, but only when his platoon had filed its winding way up a final communication trench into the front line was he really 'in the line'. Many thousands of troops serving in France, for quite proper reasons, never achieved the dangerous elitism of having served in the line. Some never approached it, their duties keeping them at the Bases or on the Lines of Communication. Some, charged with maintaining supplies to forward positions, had regular hazardous journeys to make up to the line. Some, on construction or maintenance tasks, had spells in the line, but on the infantry battalion officers and men rests the thorny accolade of having 'held the line'. It must be stated that an Artillery battery in action, perhaps particularly a field artillery battery under counter-battery fire, could in its emplacement well consider its lot as having a close kinship to the front line soldier and additionally such a battery would have a presence in the line, or even ahead of it, in a forward sap. This would be the forward artillery observation officer and his signaller or signallers.

We need to be mindful of more than the soldier's duty in the line. Enemy mine, U boat or destroyer brought to the sailor whose ship patrolled the North Sea, the Channel, the Atlantic, the Mediterranean or even further afield, his own very different 'front line' experience. It was one where the strain could be prolonged, though actual engagement with the enemy infrequent. It is tempting with khaki in mind to balance against the nervous tension of North Sea patrolling the likelihood of good food, of reasonable shipboard and good shore accommodation and of leave prospects, but all this would be relative. Scapa Flow in winter was a picnic for no one. It might be added, too, that North Sea destroyer service experience, in physical terms, would be strikingly different from that of the more comfortable existence in a huge Dreadnought.

For the airman, that is the actual pilots and observers, 'over the line' experience was again in a technological framework and one more fallible than that of the sailor. This fallibility, from take-off to return landing, provided an additional element of uncertainty to the accumulated opposition from ground and air as the airman attempted to carry out his task. As the air war evolved and specialization of task and machine developed with increasing sophistication, airmen were arguably in a position of more constant immediacy of danger than that of any other servicemen. If it were countered that the Battle of Loos, or the first day on the Somme, or the Autumn months of the attack in the Ypres Salient make such a statement wholly inappropriate, then the rejoinder would be that the airmen suffered their fearful losses too, of which April and May, 1917, were but the most notorious.

To return to the soldier, it is important to shun ideas of unrelenting torment of shelling, of the ferocity of constant attack and counterattack. Any picture of almost continuous battle and unceasing bombardment is wildly exaggerated. The idea of boredom is less easy to grasp, but, unless we are aware of it, we miss an element of the soldier's experience. Squalor, the impact of which would be affected by weather and ground conditions, is easier to picture. With the sheer, cold misery of prolonged rain there came the practical problems caused by collapsing trenches, flooded dugouts, latrine pits or overturned latrine tins adding their contents to the liquid mud which would first render the duckboards of limited use and then obscure them altogether if the lie of the land were an additional enemy. In a winter like that of 1916–17, temperatures fell so low that entrenching tools rang with loud ineffectuality on iron-hard ground when a new sap or tunnel construction was needed. In summer, to add to flies and lice and fleas, there were the all-pervading smells, dirt, damp, decay, chloride of lime and the distinctive stench of bodies disinterred by shelling or of those killed whose remains could not be buried.

Endurance of such unpleasantness was for limited periods. A new unit would take over its designated sector at night and usually hold it for four to six days before being relieved. There were of course many occasions when the period was prolonged. The photographs in this section illustrate the different conditions which could obtain in a front-line trench and at the same time give an idea

of the depth of a trench, the mandatory firestep, parapet and par-
ados. In certain areas, sandbagged and timbered breastworks had to
be erected because the high water table of the ground precluded the
digging of trenches. The clutter of equipment, the boxes of
ammunition, the excavated dugouts, the wickerwork and timber
side-supports, the duckboard footing, the traverses, all these
elements would soon be familiar to the soldier in the line. The rats
too would long be remembered by the soldier. Here they are not
pictured in their legendary size, simply in numbers. In the orderly
ranks of their dead, so different from their shadowy gleaming-eyed
scurrying presence in nocturnal life, their evil reputation is unwar-
rantably diminished.

Sentries from the firestep, perhaps using a trench periscope or
listening from a forward sap, were on constant alert against enemy
movements. Snipers sought their own personal harvest through
steel loopholes. At night, patrols moved out through carefully
arranged gaps in the defending apron of barbed wire to gather
intelligence of enemy activity. Wiring parties improved existing
work while beneath all this, if the ground were suitable, sappers
wormed tunnels towards the enemy positions for preparation of
explosive charges to be electrically detonated, destroying the posi-

tions above and leaving a crater to be stormed by the assault troops. If successful, the troops would build up the forward lip of the crater into a new extension of the British lines.

On occasion an attempt by a body of troops silently to cross No-Man's-Land at night would be followed by an outbursting maelstrom of murderous activity. It would be for the capture of prisoners or even to take a particularly troublesome sector of the enemy positions. To add to the immediate racket of small arms fire, shouts, thuds, screams, the explosion of hand-grenades, the racing skywards of German S.O.S. rockets, there would in all probability be the deafening overture of artillery co-operation and indirect machine-gun fire to box in the beleaguered German defenders. Naturally the reverse of this situation could develop with a terrifying suddenness for the men holding a British part of the line.

There were long quiet periods too, and some areas outside of the priorities of opposing High Command intention seemed to have had, accidentally or by intent, an informal live-and-let-live arrangement. It would continue until disturbed by external decision. In these areas, and indeed to some extent in all, routine regimented daily life from 'stand to', an hour before daylight, to

Holding the line at a quiet time could be wearisomely uncomfortable and boring as seems to be indicated by this picture of Royal Fusiliers in trenches running through a still recognisable wood early in 1915. The presence of a heavy duty pump and the markedly raised duckboards are clear indications of one prevailing problem. (*Captain K. W. Brewster, 1st Bn, Royal Fusiliers*)

that same inspected readiness an hour before dark. The morning issue of rum in the presence of an officer, the doling out from sandbags of bread, tins of stew or bully beef, biscuits, tea, sugar, condensed milk, bacon to be fried in a mess tin, letters, perhaps for a lucky man even a parcel, these were the highlights of the day. Time would be spent in maintaining a rifle in an efficient state and in keeping to whatever personal or trench tidiness local conditions allowed and to the standard which local command required. In this way a quiet day would be passed but always under the protection of the outward scrutiny of the sentries.

For men moving up to the line for battle assault there was greatly increased tension, but even in this, as certainly in all other trench-holding circumstances, we should be aware of a man's distinctively individual emotional response to his current situation. As some men were deeply depressed and indeed felt foredoomed on the eve of battle, others might be more fatalistic or composed, numbed or by contrast frustrated with pent-up exhilaration. The need to conceal inner fear from others was felt by everyone but by none more so than those who held any rank. This testing time for the young subaltern burdened him heavily with the responsibility of leadership but by the same token gave him the self-control he needed. To fail before one's own men was so unthinkable that it was a pit of degradation from which almost all successfully held back. Of the discarding of fear, of the exultation in battle, of the freedom of leaving the tomb of the trench, of the rage and savagery of action, the numbing of the senses, the insufficiency of time to think and then of the later relief at having come through, of the retching revulsion at what had been seen or done, the headache and the exhaustion – these and other emotions were caught in contemporary evidence as well as by later recall. Few sentences in a letter emphasize in higher relief the almost inevitable incomprehension we may have in grasping the feeling of an experience beyond our personal imagination than "the whole show was packed full of interest and was I think the best I've been in yet and that's saying something". The sentence concludes a vivid account of killing the enemy in close combat. No generalization could possibly be made from this, none is suggested, but it might serve as a caution against generalizations totally at variance with it.

The direction of the war commitment of some women conferred upon them what they would have considered the privilege of nursing war wounded and sick and this brought them to some extent into contact with the soldier's experience of the line. In addition to the professionally trained and experienced nurses in Army, Territorial or other organizations, a considerable army of volunteers in the emergency of war undertook training or extended existing First Aid qualifications and experience and offered themselves for service in War Hospitals at home and overseas. There was a range of duties for them to undertake, but those who were to specialize in ambulance-driving or ward-nursing were to come close to the suffering endured by men at war. The background of Voluntary Aid Detachment nurses was usually that of the middle or upper middle class in so far as such designations have anything other than a general meaning, but the widening of their experience of life by tending to the needs of men quite irrespective of their social origin was immeasurably and permanently enriching. The concept of service pulsed strongly in these women and would be reanimated a generation later without the need of conscription. A realization of this helps us to appreciate the remarkable ease with which they accommodated themselves to tasks wholly beyond their prior vision. Once again one is faced with what may be unwelcome – that a sense of social responsibility, of community, of humanity, of fellowship, is excited by the awfulness of war in a way which only a natural disaster can generate in peacetime. Not incidentally it may even be that this extension of the numbers of women involved in nursing, or the nature of that nursing, played its part, with the related mix of the sexes in munitions factories or shipyards, in working towards the equalization of male and female relationships, certainly a positive result of the war.

Opposite March 1916, Neuville St Vaast sector. Men of the 5th Battalion, South Staffordshire Regiment, having taken over trenches from the French, find weather conditions and the maintenance standard of the previous occupants combining against them. The more fortunate soldiers have waders to keep their feet dry. Two men are wearing the recently issued steel helmets. (*F. Wilkinson*)

Lieutenant Horsfield (extreme left), of the Royal Field Artillery, visits Vimy Ridge front line positions in May, 1916, which are being held by the 8th Battalion Border Regiment. The fixed bayonet on the rifles provides evidence that this was a sector when it was seldom 'all quiet'. (*William Aitchison*)

Men of the 6th Battalion, Royal Fusiliers in
the line near Armentières in the Spring of
1915. Their trench is well-constructed with
a wooden firestep serving as a very
reasonable seat. Quite extraordinarily, two
examples of framed art work (presumably
from nearby shell-damaged empty houses)
give a homely touch to a section of the
Western Front where at the moment all
does seem quiet.
*(K. W. Brewster, 6th Battalion, Royal
Fusiliers)*

The problem of drainage: 1.5.15. Royal Engineers have provided a pump to deal with flooding in a trench occupied by the Cameronians. A Cameronian officer, the donor of this photograph, had suggested that the pump would be of limited use as the water could not be encouraged to run uphill despite his men having spent long stints on pumping fatigue. The trench led to a dugout, Battalion HQ, which the Commanding Officer and the Adjutant regularly had to bale out until they gave up and sat with their feet on the table. The only answer here proved to be the building of a breastwork. (*Major-General R. C. Money, at that time 1st Battalion, Cameronians*)

32.

strain was too much for him.

At 29 minutes past seven the next morning it was dead still – and one minute later with a deafening crash every gun in the area loosed off simultaneously and for 35 minutes it seemed as if all the Devils in Hell were let loose as the world fell to pieces with thunderous crashes. The earth shook & vibrated incessantly & twelve guns belching hell close to my dugout only added to the noise as it were blows in a boxing match.

The regiment had the honour of being the first to attack and at 8·0c the Company Commanders began to call out the minutes. 5 – 4 – 3 – 2 – 1.

At 8 also I sent my stretcher bearers to pick up the casualties from the open over which they had to charge but there was so much to be done inside the parapet we did not get out for a bit.

The show began for me when I got the message "Capt. Morgan is hit & is bleeding badly".

A Medical Officer's contemporary account of the Battle of Neuve Chapelle, 10–13 March, 1915. It had been his responsibility to establish a Regimental Aid Post in the front line trench from which the assaulting infantry had attacked. The Medical Officer, Captain E. C. Deane RAMC, attached to the 2nd Leicesters, was himself to be killed on the eve of the Battle of Loos in late September that same year. (*Captain E. C. Deane*)

I ran along the trenches to him fearful of finding a shattered wreck. Doubling round traverses. jumping over pools of blood. severed limbs with no owners. shattered corpses & groaning wounded.

A Gurkha with his right hand handed me his left arm torn off above the elbow & wailed Sahib! Sahib! and as I ran on I heard a Jock say "Nice bloody Doctor wouldn't treat a wounded man."

Morgan seemed shrunk to about half his usual size & was very blue. 5 wounds mostly in the lung & probably our own shell.

I had him taken off across the open & he is probably doing well – anyhow I've seen him since & he was fine then.

Coming back men lay in pools of blood where it had been quite open before on the way out.

After this there was a nightmare of bandaging & Iodine & blood – always blood. Working in the dugout with bent back all day

The only way in which looking 'over the top' could be done with any measure of security was by means of a trench periscope. Here a simple box variety is being demonstrated from rear positions. (*Brigadier H. L. Graham, 6th Battalion, South Staffordshire Regiment*)

Opposite Sniping activity under local authority could be undertaken by men of any rank. Here, in a reserve position near Armentières during 1915, an officer poses with his rifle equipped with a telescopic sight. (*K. W. Brewster*)

Men of the 6th Battalion, Royal Fusiliers prepare their barbed wire for the protection of the approach to their trench. The coils will be taken into No-Man's-Land at night and wound through or round the loops in iron picquets which had to be screwed into the ground as silently as possible – difficult and dangerous work. (*K. W. Brewster*)

Men of a tunnelling company of Royal Engineers mine their way forward under Messines Ridge for the eventual placement and detonation of the 21 charges (two failing in the event) in the early hours of 7 June, 1917. It appears as if one of the men was responsible for digging a tunnel laterally from the main shaft in order to listen for any German counter-mining. If necessary, explosive charges would be set to destroy the enemy work. (*From a set of commercially produced stereoscopic slides*)

1st Battalion, Cameronians HQ Officers' Mess in the line, 18 November, 1914. The Commanding Officer, Colonel Robertson, is to the left, the Regimental Medical Officer, Lieutenant Davidson, is in the centre and on the right is Captain Sam Darling. (*Major-General R.C. Money*)

Two machine gunners of the Royal
Fusiliers in the front line near Armentières
in the summer of 1915. The gun is the
belt-fed Vickers Mark I. One end of the
canvas belt can be seen hanging out of the
left-hand side of the gun, which is fired by
pressing on the thumb trigger between the
'spade' grips. Introduced in 1912, the
Vickers gun was of such utility that it
remained in Army service until 1965.
(*K. W. Brewster*)

Left A soldier in Roman or Medieval times
would have recognized the weapon of siege
warfare photographed here. Catapults of
various designs were employed in small
number on the Western Front and at
Gallipoli. The version shown here, using
elastic as the propellant, would hurl a locally
improvised charge the 120 feet or so across
No-Man's-Land into the enemy trenches at
Frelinghien near Armentières in 1915.
(*B. H. Church, RFA*)

Opposite Winter sunlight illuminating a
Cameronian dugout where 2nd Lieutenant
C. D. W. Rooke copies out a map of the local
trench system for Brigade HQ, 18.11.14.
The Cameronians had just moved into
these positions on the Lys near Frelinghien.
The donor of the photograph, an officer in
the same battalion as Rooke, has written:
"These were 'cushy' trenches and we were
hardly ever shelled". The explanation was
that immediately behind the Germans, who
were about 90 yards away, were high
buildings which blocked the enemy guns
from ranging on the British front line.
(*Major-General R. C. Money*)

THURSDAY, April 22, 1915.

) 3.39 pm.   {112—253

Up for dinner in Pyjamas. Have a look round the
Dugouts. Write letter, censor the men's, have tea 8"
A terrific bombardment starts during the afternoon.
Aeroplanes all over the place A.A Guns very busy. Star
rockets going up in the distance. Get my party off
at 7 but before I go an Artillery Major gives orders for
us to stand to. We hear the Boshs have asphyxiated the
French with their Gas shells, & many small parties have
broken through. Canadians stand & hold them. The whole
place is in an uproar. Now Germans are in Wietije.
All our kits are packed for a moments move. We're all rather
worried. Ypres is in flames in many places. Shells
keep on bursting just behind us, & the bits & pieces fly
around us. Just as I write a man has come in to say
a horse has been hit outside by a bit of the last one
over. The rifle fire is terrific — & machine guns
make things worse. . .
The Turcos come flying through the village in a
panic, terror in their faces, with tales of the cursed
gas shells — many are wounded. Villagers with
their children & household goods make one long
stream of wailing humanity.
The Gas from the shells made our eyes smart
& run with water, & we were at least 3 miles
away. No bed for me & no sleep —

4.5⅟
7·5 FRIDAY, April 23, 1915. ✓ **11·21 ~** **2·2~ ~**

[113—252]   St. George.

P calls me up soon after 5ᴏ⅟ with message from the
Major. We have to go down at once – No breakfast –
And now I have a morning I shall remember for
many a long day. They start shelling our huts, billets
+ horse lines. The awful suspense, as these awful tearing
sounds come screaming through the air. Nearer + Nearer.
Every one rushes to a steep bank for shelter, + in it we start
digging ourselves dug-outs, 6'across + about 9' in – with
2' of earth on top, supported by timber from wrecked houses.
And all the time shells continue to fall. we shrink into
the places we dig & wait for the burst. When things quieten
down we get on the higher ground to see what has:
happened. Huge holes in the dry earth 8 & 10 feet across + 4 or 5
deep. But of those that have found other billets ————
Just the otherside of the road – only a few yards from where
we took shelter are 6 dead horses – +2 men – The injured
have been taken away – one shell only – Both men + horses
were Wessex Signal Cᵒ – Other shells found other victims.
     How one's heart aches to hear the poor little children
shriek with terror as they hear the shells come, + burst – as
they hurry along the road to safety – laden with loads
that are heavy even for grown ups. 'Tis a painful
subject this. I am off on the 2ᵈ line trenches after
a meagre lunch of bully & bread – Work till 8·30 + then
back to the dug outs without food, or blankets – War
is a hard life truly. The rifle fire is hard at it once
again. What does it mean, + when will it end?

The city of Ypres under shellfire and the
opening of a German attack using gas. This
Royal Engineer officer's diary account is
truly remarkable in its graphic description
of a developing military emergency in a city
still holding its civilian occupants. "How
one's heart aches to hear the poor little
children shriek with terror as they hear the
shells come." (N. C. Harbutt)

A face of war: Two officers of the Royal Scots Fusiliers pose on 18 March, 1916, for a behind-the-line studio portrait with and without their recently issued gas protection helmets. In a letter written in May of that year the donor of this photograph wrote not of gas but of being near an exploding German mortar: "There was just a faint 'pouff' from t'other side, a parabola formed by a trail of sparks. A short prayer from me. Then about half a second (it seemed ages) of appalling suspense, a 'swish thud', another eternity, an appalling roar. Head half-jerked off shoulders, face scorched, hair singed, steel helmet badly scored." (*Major-General Sir Edmund Hakewill Smith, on the left of the photograph*)

A 60-pounder gun of the 153rd Heavy Battery, Royal Garrison Artillery, in action on the Macedonian Front. The gun has just been fired; two of the gunners have a covering hand to an ear. This artillery piece had a range of 10,300 yards and a rate of fire of just over two rounds a minute. (R. W. Stenhouse, RGA)

A 4.5-inch howitzer emplaced and in action above the Anzac beachhead on the Gallipoli Peninsula in 1915. The gunners are New Zealanders of an artillery brigade recruited from Otago. (E. A. Burrows, RN)

An American Tank Unit (No 301) entraining its British supplied Mark V tanks at Saulty railhead late in 1918. (S. Horscroft, No 8 Squadron RAF, co-operating with tanks)

American soldiers await orders to go forward in the Allied advance to victory in 1918. The soldiers are equipped with British Lee Enfield rifles. Tank exhaust fumes shroud the scene but ahead of the Americans an Australian peers into the gloom. Note the field telephone wires in the foreground. (*A. H. Kynaston, RFA*)

A more comfortable way to move up to the line, but here, in the harsh conditions of the Sinai between Egypt and Palestine, there was both reason and opportunity for soldiers to travel by open wagon in a goods train. A flat car, in this instance, seems to offer some uncluttered space for the mixed regimental group of officers and NCOs in the foreground. (*W. Hairsine, East Riding Imperial Yeomanry*)

The end of the line? An accident on the turntable at Jerusalem presents something of a problem to this Royal Engineer workgang.

The upturned engine had an unusual history: it was German, had been captured on the high seas, landed for full assembly at Cardiff and was then shipped out to Egypt to support the British advance on Gaza and from thence into Palestine.

(*G. D. Breffitt, RE*)

Gun drill for ratings of the destroyer HMS *Lurcher*, probably in early 1917. Caps are secured by chinstraps for this exercise. Nearest to the camera, the sightsetter is training one of *Lurcher's* two four-inch guns. (*P. H. F. Haig-Ferguson, HMS Lurcher*)

A different sort of line and one which moved. Astern of the Dreadnought battleship HMS *Queen Elizabeth*, battleships of the Grand Fleet carry out a sweep into the North Sea. (*Admiral Sir T. H. Binney, at that time an officer in HMS* Queen Elizabeth)

HMS *Royal Sovereign* of the 1st Battle
Squadron based at Rosyth is framed by the
Forth Bridge. A Dreadnought battleship
launched in 1915 and with a main armament
of eight 15-inch guns, *Royal Sovereign* went
on to serve in the Second World War and
was loaned for service with the Soviet
Russian Navy between 1944 and 1949 as the
Archangelsk. (*Vice Admiral J. S. C. Salter, at
that time with HMS* Ramillies)

Inside the great natural harbour Naval base
of Scapa Flow in the Orkneys. The
submarine is a G class vessel used for
coastal patrol, one of only fourteen built. In
the background are three Dreadnought
battleships, left to right, HMS *Orion*, HMS
Barham and HMS *Collingwood*, all of which
were present at the Battle of Jutland in 1916.
(*G. Foster Hall, HMS* Collingwood)

In the search for war-related goods – 'contraband' en route for Germany – a boarding party is sent from HMS *Swiftsure* to a fully rigged sailing vessel in the South Atlantic in April, 1916. The whaler with the boarding party can be seen close by the ship's stern. (*E. T. W. Church, HMS* Swiftsure)

Merchantman in the line of duty. The last moments of the SS *Worcestershire*, sinking after she had struck a mine in the Indian Ocean ten miles south-west of Colombo on 17 February, 1917. This Bibby Line vessel sank with the loss of two lives. (*W. Shearer, HMS* Cornwall)

1915 in the Sea of Marmara and the Royal Navy submarine *E11* has captured several small Turkish sailing vessels. The crews from all these craft (caiques) are being assembled aboard the one which will remain undestroyed. *E11*'s achievements in these enemy waters led to the award of the Victoria Cross to her Captain, Lieutenant-Commander M. E. Nasmith. (*E. L. Berthon, HMS* Raccoon)

The aircraft carrier HMS *Pegasus*, attached to the Grand Fleet, was capable of a speed of 20 knots, insufficient in fact to allow her to operate effectively in such company. Here, in August, 1918, in her dazzle camouflage, she is seen in the Firth of Forth. *Pegasus* carried nine landplanes stowed in the aft deck hangar and launched off the ramp seen at the bow. (*Dr W. Gover, HMS* Fearless)

HMS *Inflexible* has struck a mine. She has taken a list to port and is in danger of sinking, but fiddles come to the fore in this emergency. The battlecruiser is under shell fire from the shore and a collision mat needs to be lowered over a gaping rent. Two Marine bandsmen provide a tuneful tempo to bring unison to the efforts of the ratings manning the capstan. (*Rear Admiral B. Sebastian, then in HMS* Inflexible.)

An event in a Boxing tournament aboard the Pre-Dreadnought battleship HMS *Swiftsure*, March, 1916, about which time she left the Eastern Mediterranean for service in the South Atlantic. (*E. T. W. Church*)

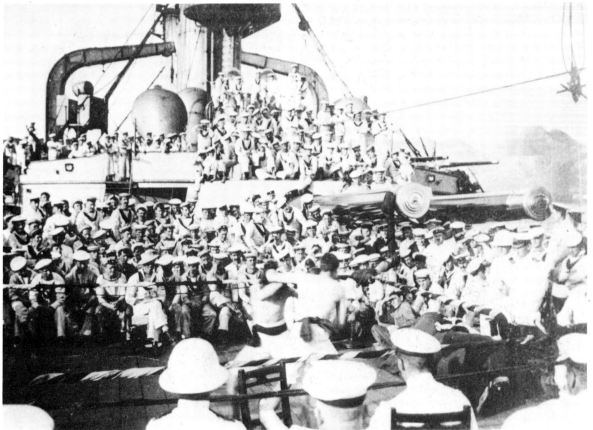

Pilots and Observers of No 10 Squadron RAF at Droglandt aerodrome in the spring of 1918. Standing in front of the Bristol Fighter, reserved by the unit for special missions, are, from left to right, Storrs, Williams, Hughes, Burdick, Middleton, Churchman, Jackson, Slattery, Bowen and Clark. (*C. E. Townley, Suffolk Regiment, attached RAF*)

134

Above the line. A British observation balloon looms above its handling party prior to its ascent at Acq near Vimy Ridge in April, 1916. An essential but vulnerable watch over the enemy positions was conducted from the balloon's suspended basket and in particular the accuracy of British shelling of known targets could be observed. (*William Aitchison*)

The most common Army Co-operation aircraft for the British by 1918 was the RE8 with its 140 hp engine. This example, at St Omer Aircraft Depot in May, 1918, was the personal plane of Captain D. F. Stevenson, DSO, MC, seen here on his shooting stick. Stevenson was a flight commander in No 4 Squadron RAF. The photograph was probably taken to commemorate the departure of his usual observer, 2nd Lieutenant John Baker, the donor of the photograph. Baker was returning to England for pilot training after six months of flying in the back seat. Their RE8 is unusual in that they have fitted an extra machine-gun on the top wing. (*Air Chief Marshal Sir John Baker*)

Left The Dolomite Mountains of this part of the Italian/Austro Hungarian Front provide a scenically impressive setting in late 1916 for Austrian gunners of the 14th Heavy Artillery Regiment equipped with their 150 mm mortar on its firing platform. Though a soldier holds the firing lanyard, the casual stance of the others belies this as a photograph of the mortar in action. (*W. Augenfeld of this unit*)

Above German gunners on the Eastern Front. Members of 274 Field Artillery Regiment beside one of their 8 cm howitzers at Wolhynia in the Ukraine, a quiet sector in the Winter of 1917–18. Left to right, Medical Orderly Weber, *Unteroffizier* Oelsner and Gunners Höhne and Timmel. (*Dr. W. G. Oelsner*)

A Turkish standard-bearer and his escort. Among no troops was spiritual fervour a more powerful motivator than in the army of Germany's ally, the Ottoman Empire. The main fronts where British and Imperial troops confronted the Turks were on the Gallipoli Peninsula, Mesopotamia and in Egypt and Palestine. (*C. P. Carlson, Honourable Artillery Company*)

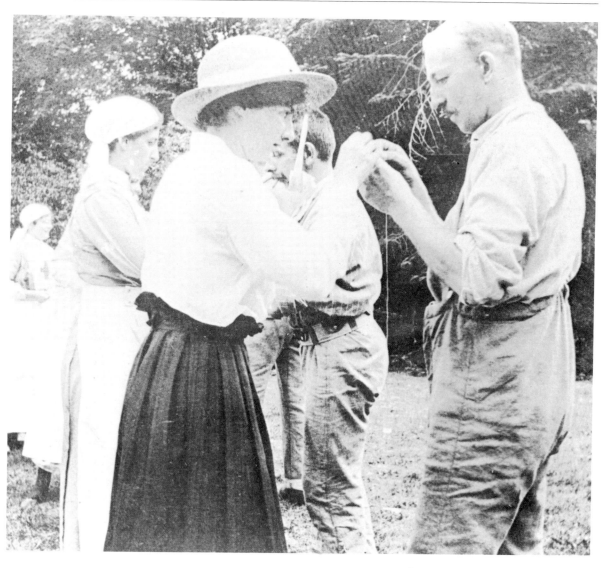

Sports Day, July, 1916, at Waverley Abbey VAD hospital in Surrey. In this needle and thread race, Nurses Trouton, Barker and Munn are shown with two patients in view, Underwood and Poole. (*Mrs May Dunlop, VAD Nurse at Waverley Abbey as Miss May Justice*)

Left Rifleman Coules of the Rifle Brigade and Private Stevenson of the 17th Battalion, Highland Light Infantry, pose in their hospital garb of blue jacket and trousers and white shirt with red tie during their convalescence in September, 1916, at Huntroyde Auxiliary Military Hospital at Padiham, Lancashire. (*Mrs Y. M. Smythe, VAD Nurse at Padiham as Miss Maxtone Graham*)

St George's Hospital
Hyde Park. Corner.
S.W. 1.
Dec: 15th 17

Dear Madam –
          I expect you
have heard from a
Military source that
your Husband is
suffering from "Tetanus".
which came on four
days ago – It is a
very painful condition
due to general stiffness.
He would like to see
you – & I would advise

you to come
arrange for
a railway
of course
day or two
& you then
can get it
refunded
.....very
your Hus...
so plucky
I should...
much a...
he cann...
sends hi...
...

"Your husband is very plucky ... I shouldn't worry too much." A Munition girl living with her husband's parents received this letter from a Hospital Sister in whose ward the girl's husband lay wounded, tetanus weakening his condition. A whole series of telegrams as well as the formal notification had told her of the fact that No 15217 Pte G. W. Fowler, 6th King's Own Scottish Borderers, was dangerously ill, suffering from gunshot wounds in the chest in No 4 General Hospital, Camiers, that she cannot visit him, then that he had been transferred to St George's Hospital, London. Before Mrs Fowler could get to London, a telegram informed her that her husband had died and then the family received a final telegram: "Remains late G. Fowler arrive Normanton 9 a.m. 20.12.17 Missed train owing to fog." (*Mrs G. W. Fowler*)

St George's Hospital
Hyde Park Corner
S.W.1
Dec. 15th, 17

Dear Madam,
   I expect you have heard from a
military source that your Husband is
suffering from Tetanus, which came
on four days ago. It is a very painful
condition due to general stiffness. He
would like to see you – and I would
advise you to come – I will arrange for
you to have a railway pass – that of
course will take a day or two to reach
you – if you start without it you can get
the money refunded to you later – I am
very sorry for your husband—he is so
plucky and very bright. I shouldn't
worry too much about him – he cannot
write – he sends his love. His surgeon
has seen him today and thinks he is
better –

Yours faithfully
Helen Hands
Sister of
MacCalmond Ward
to
Mrs Fowler

PART FOUR

Man to Man.

ONE OF the elements of military service in the Great War which has remained virtually unscathed by the literature of disillusionment of the inter-war years and the more tardy re-flowering of such writing in the 1960s is the comradeship bred among men under the variable circumstances of active service. In several senses were the circumstances variable. Here we are mostly concerned with men spending regular periods in the front line, but we should also be mindful men of experiencing very different conditions but nonetheless building up something akin to the spirit which bound men together in the trenches. Among the crew of a small submarine in the Dardanelles or the Baltic, a mutual identification in success and in survival was inevitably forged. The confinement of living and working conditions, the presence of danger in some degree, were there all the time. The maintenance of an all-round excellence of command had to be as constant as the utter reliability required of every rating in the performance of his duties. From all this there was bred a teamwork which might not protect against disaster but without which the craft could not operate successfully.

Quite different from this but certainly related to it was the working relationship holding together an air squadron in France. The differences are obvious – officers and men in separate Messes and sleeping accommodation; pilots and observers (usually but by no means always Commissioned Officers) distinctive from ground personnel – but the success of the squadron was built upon a close awareness of mutual interdependence. Unit pride and man to man respect stood at the heart of *esprit de corps* and, even in a service calling for a high degree of individualism and greatly dependent upon technology, *esprit de corps* had an important part to play.

It may not be an attractive word but 'mateship' has been used to

Opposite At six foot, eleven and a half, Captain Hay of the Black Watch was reputedly the tallest man in the British Army. Here, at Le Touret in France, he is pictured with fellow Black Watch officer, Jack Scott. On 9 April, 1915, not long after the taking of this photograph, Scott was killed leading his men into attack at the Battle of Aubers Ridge. (*J. G. Scott*)

describe the basic ingredient of good unit morale. By extension we may conclude that, on whatever other elements the fighting or endurance quality of the nine hundred or so men in a battalion rests, it is fundamentally founded upon the close-knit fellowship of tiny groups of men within the greater number. The fellowship must extend to the other groups, but each nucleus, being bound together by the refusal of any one of its constituent elements even to consider letting the others down, could ensure the cohesive strength of the whole. To fight for, to protect and to be protected by one's mates; to share with, to stick in with, to uphold one's place with one's mates; when such attitudes animate the groups within the sections, platoons and companies of a battalion, its Commanding Officer is fortunate. It may be added that he and his officers would almost certainly have earned their place within these fierce loyalties, however distinctive their place by rank.

Articulating the higher emotions is unlikely to be common in the ordinary soldier's correspondence other than in matters relating to loving relationships with those at home. Indeed when officers or men write with any philosophical profundity or literary felicity about the strength of masculine loyalties holding them together through time of stress, the modern reader, aware that he is in the presence of a sort of love, may instinctively feel uncomfortable. Whether influenced by scepticism or by distaste for the unfortunate modern connotations of the vocabulary, he cannot easily identify with the sentiment, or, as seems to be the case with a regrettably well-known American professor dabbling in the subject, wholly misunderstands what he reads.

Men received and gave comfort, cheer, support and strength in their comradeship. They achieved humour through it and by their comradeship their grumbling could be expressed with healthy satisfaction. The grousing but sardonically humorous soldier is a universal figure, but one planted on fertile soil in France during the First World War. It is worth reminding ourselves that the only other escape from the trials of the soldiers actually in the line, that of outright mutiny, was not taken by any British units at the front. We need not look for a complete explanation for this in the inviolable efficiency and draconian retribution of British Military discipline as it is far more complex. Comradeship was a vital ingredient on both sides of No-Man's-Land so perhaps no special claims can be made for the efficacy of the British brand. Material superiority is obviously a hugely important factor in determining the maintenance of morale in a long struggle for victory, but if the human factor be granted any importance and we may not claim anything special for the British soldier's morale, we may have to give some credence to the idea of superior British Generalship, or that the Allies simply had a better cause, and that really would be food for thought!

In peacetime a man was offered the twin environment of his home and his workplace in which to establish his identity. Their attractions, repulsions or lack of impact would mould both the inner man and his outward presentation of himself. The insularity of Army life, and certainly of the line, provided no such opportunity. The trench was no place for privacy, little of the inner man could be hidden there and an artificial front would be known for what it was. Thoughts might remain unspoken but silence still carried messages readily interpreted. Looks exchanged, gestures made, deeds done or undone, the long talk or the regular brief exchange, this was the currency by which man measured man. As one old soldier observed to the author recently, "We knew each other's strength and weaknesses and accepted them."

There was a sad irony about this positive quality of mutual understanding. It was exclusive, and, for a multitude of reasons at the time and since, it was not to be shared with the folks at home.

Men of the West Lancashire Field Ambulance (T.F.) in their billeting barn at Westerham in Kent, May, 1915. Even in the relaxed informality of the gathering, a fair amount of polishing is under way. This unit is destined for the Cape Helles beachhead, Gallipoli. (*A. P. Pickthall, RAMC*)

Many were the wives and mothers who found communication difficult with their loved ones on leave. They resented their husband's or son's unwillingness to talk of things in France, could not comprehend that such unwillingness was harnessed to incapacity. Long silences or dismissively monosyllabic answers to earnest questions were distressing. In some sense this exclusion proved interminable as women-folk through succeeding decades put up with their man's commitment to the all-male world of the old comrades' association activities. Some women did go with their husbands on pilgrimage to France but this was a departure from the norm and it would be nice to know if the animated chatter of husband's explanation and description to wife were punctuated by the old awkward silences.

It should be added here that women also established their right to a wartime sistership of overseas service. In France particularly, and quite apart from nurses and ambulance drivers, the Women's Legion and then the Women's Army Auxiliary Corps provided valuable substitute labour for the support of the Army. Cooks, waitresses, clerks, laundresses, typists, driver mechanics and telephonists were among the occupational vacancies. The opportunity thus afforded for working-class women to undertake service in uniform overseas was a noteworthy step in the achievement of enhanced self-respect and the claim that men must reappraise a woman's independent worth. As one looks at photographs of women cheerfully engaged in the adventure of their overseas service, it is worth remembering that in the Base Camps, in the hospitals and casualty clearing stations, they would be subject to long-range shelling and, by First World War standards, heavy air raids. Some women would be wounded, some lose their lives, some decorated for their conduct under dangerous circumstances. Not the least of the satisfaction for one smiling lady was the honour of a paybook entry identical with that of a soldier: paid 'In the Field'.

Under circumstances of working partnership or of traditional custom, as with the sailor and the Ship's Cat, war did not interrupt the close affinity some men felt for animals. It is most natural to see the development of this in the interdependence of a working partnership like that of the man with mules bringing up ammunition or the mounted gunner with a team of horses drawing an artillery limber. The relationship could be less intimate and involve a group rather than an individual. So protectively affectionate did one artillery battery feel for its adopted mascot, a stray dog, that a miniature steel helmet was made for their pet. At another extreme, by number and variety, a photograph held in the Archives shows the pets of an

RFC Squadron with a line-up of a chicken, a fox cub, a rabbit, a Jack Russell terrier, two cats, a puppy and a pig. It has to be admitted that there was an element of eccentricity in that Squadron (No 42 at Bailleul in 1917) in that a white picket mini-fence on the same photograph marks the grave of the Mess piano mortally injured during the course of a party.

With the comradeship of man, and occasionally of animal, as an integral part of service life, we are left to consider whether relationships with the enemy were of any significance beyond the exceptional circumstances of a truce or the exchange of verbal or visual badinage from closely proximate trench positions.

The seldom-seen nearness of the German bred curiosity and respect. It is not surprising that khaki opinions of the enemy were not in accord with the overheated venom of those expressed at home. There is, however, certainly evidence from first to last of the British soldier's lack of trust of the German. Such suspicions are aired with conclusive vehemence, but the wounded opponent could also excite pity in the aftermath of action. In the line, linked by the very swathe of wired fire-zone which separated them, there was some mutual sympathy in a shared dangerous existence and overall the Tommy could not help but respect his foe's soldierly qualities. It remains a matter of some embarrassment that he was not so ready to accord the same respect to his allies whose efforts were rewarded with scant acknowledgement. We ought not really to be surprised that 19th century British condescension to 'less fortunate' people was in the 20th century being replaced by a more defensive position of moderate chauvinist disparagement of even our friends.

Men of No 10 Platoon of the 6th
Battalion, South Staffordshire Regiment,
in support positions near Armentières
in the spring of 1915. The photographer
was their subaltern, H. L. Graham.
(*Brigadier H. L. Graham*)

'A bombing party': An officer and his team of hand-grenade throwers from the 8th Battalion, Border Regiment, in an advanced post, Vimy Ridge, May, 1916. In this part of the line the opposing trenches were very close so that a post forward of the line was especially perilous even without the further consideration of the honeycomb of passages, of mine and counter-mine tunnels and German mine activity beneath the feet of the men photographed here. (*W. Aitchison*)

Teamwork essential: A Royal Field Artillery 18 pdr in action at Houplines on 7 December, 1914. The gunner to the left is adjusting the time setting of the fuse. (*Major General R.C. Money*)

A German trench at Givenchy captured by
the 1st Battalion, Black Watch, on 25
January and photographed on the following
day. The men whose faces are shown here
had been involved in two days of intense
fighting which involved attack and
counterattack, the loss and recapture of
this 1st line trench.
(*J. G. Scott of this battalion*)

A wounded German being attended to by his
enemy at the March, 1915, Battle of Neuve
Chapelle. His captors are men of the 41st
Dogras, Indian Army, but there is a French
soldier present too. (*C. A. M. Dunlop,
Dogras*)

No. 1324 Pte Devonshire
B. E. F. Infantry Base Depot
France
22/1/15

Dear Sir,

I received your address from Mr. Mitchell whom you had asked to go ...

First of all I sincerely hope you are recovering from your wounds and that you will soon be able to get about. It was so unfortunate for you to be one paralysed, or rather so, you or you will otherwise ... our Company and the 1st figure ... waiting for you some time. ... about 10 days after the change I can understand that ...

... I think our Doctor did as well as any books could have done. No, thank you. It was a long way to ...

... progressing. ... I don't suppose there is any prospect of your being put for active service again, seeing you were hit so badly. How I got through I shall never know. Until I got this ...
mind anything else.

I shall be glad to ...

This and the following two pages "You will doubtless know our company lost all its officers ... I lost most of my pals there ... I was so sorry to see you fall at our head." Two men, survivors of the 9th Devons attack at the Battle of Loos on 25 September, 1915, write to the wounded convalescent officer who had been in command of their platoon. (*J. Pocock, the wounded subaltern*)

No. 11334 9th Devon Regt
No 7, Infantry Base Depot
Le Havre,
France
22/11/15
Dear Sir,

    I received your address from Mrs. Mitchell whom you had asked to forward it on to me.

    First of all I sincerely hope you are recovering from your wounds and that you will soon be able to get about. It was so unfortunate for you to be hit particularly so early on, for as you will doubtless know our company lost all its officers.

    I have been away from the Battalion for some time. It was about 10 days after the charge that our M.O. sent me to Hospital, and I was at Versailles for nearly five weeks. I came through the attack alright but had two slight doses of gas from them, one on the Saturday night and again on Sunday. However it was not until some days after that I felt the worst of it when I was "packed off".

    Well, Sir, I think the Devons did as well as any troops could have done, don't you. It was a long way to drive through and we were knocked up when we were checked in front of the village. I came across Elmer and Rossen when we were holding the line, and at night when we reformed Harries A joined us, so there were four of No. 5 together, but again we soon lost sight of each other.

    There was a small draft waiting for the Battalion when it left the trenches and we had one night out and went in again. As far as I can understand the 8th and 9th are relieving each other, I believe they are pretty full strength. I am waiting to go up again and shall be more at home there than here. Sgt Dearsley is here he left the Battalion a few weeks before our attack. Sgts. Williams and James have joined the Batt. since the attack: they were at Bethune while it was on.

    It was a terrible price to pay with our Brigade for that advance don't you think so sir. I lost most of my pals there, but I cannot understand how so many died, for a good many of them were wounded alongside me. I am inclined to think they kept the fire on our wounded and so killed them.

    I was so sorry to see you fall at our head, but very glad to find you are home and progressing. I don't suppose there is any prospect of you being fit for Active Service again, seeing you were hit so badly. How I got through I shall never know. Still I got there and didn't mind anything else. I shall be glad to get back again for I would just as well be there, as down here. It will feel strange with a new officer when I get back and I feel very sorry to have lost you as also the old members of the platoon.

    It is very cold out here but dry, which is one good thing, although the trenches are in a bad state there just now.

    Well sir, I shall be very pleased to learn how you are progressing, and sincerely hope you will speedily recover.

    It was hard lines on Cpl. Harvey to have been killed but his death was instantaneous. Sgt. Hawkes has been wounded recently with shrapnel and gone to England.

    Sgt Pattenden was quite alright when I last heard from up the line.

    This is all at present

        With Very Best Wishes,
        Believe me, Dear Sir,
        Yours faithfully,
        F. W. Hardy

Pte C Trouse
Nº 12247
Signal Section
9th Devons
B.E.F. France

Dear Sir

Many thanks for your kind letter
and parcel received today & am pleased
to hear you are quite well as it leaves
me just now

I am extremely obliged to you for
your kindness in sending me that parcel
which greatly appreciated not only because of
its value but mostly in which it proves
your kinds thoughts for the chaps who
were under your command.

There are very few left of the old
and original platoon about half a dozen
the remainder consisting of new drafts.

The reason I was not transferred to
another platoon is because I am in the
signal section which now together
with the bombers and Machine

Gunners constitute the Headquarter Coy under the command of Mr Hodgson.

I suppose you have heard by now that Mr Smythe & Mr Hodgson have both received the Military Cross and three men have been awarded the D.C.M.

I must now conclude with Kindest respects & wishing you a speedy recovery & best luck & wishes for 1916

I remain
Yours Obediently Sir
C Trouse.

A man and his horse: Trooper Crispin of the East Riding Imperial Yeomanry holds the reins of a real thoroughbred, 'Blacksmith', by 'Hackensmidt' out of 'Blue Veil' foaled in 1909 and serving with this Territorial unit in England, Egypt and Palestine. This fine animal was killed at Naane on 14 November, 1917. Crispin himself was to die in France in 1918. (*Brigadier M. Sykes, at that time ERIY*)

Above left Men of the 27th Punjabi Regiment, Indian Army, enjoy a traditional athletic pastime. The man on the left won this particular wrestling bout in October, 1916, somewhere along the banks of the River Tigris in Mesopotamia. (*C. R. S. Pitman, 27th Punjabis*)

Left With French civilians looking on, men of the Army Service Corps pose with their Foden 5-ton steam wagon. This heavy lorry with its cast iron wheels and solid rubber tyres became the standard vehicle of its type, the Army having eight hundred on strength in 1918. (*P. H. L. Archives*)

'Jane' takes exercise on one of the guns of Y turret, HMS *Queen Elizabeth* while this new battleship is in harbour at Mudros in the Eastern Mediterranean just prior to supporting the April, 1915 Gallipoli landings. (*Admiral Sir T. H. Binney, then of HMS* Queen Elizabeth)

Ratings of HMS *Benbow* preparatory to a sailing race of battleship launches in Scapa Flow. Such races provided exercise and entertainment and also developed teamwork and competitive spirit. (*H. M. Burrows, HMS* Benbow)

The Atlantic bridged. American battleships arriving in Scapa Flow in early December, 1917, to form the 6th Battle Squadron of the British Grand Fleet. The nearest American vessel is the USS *Texas* and she is being cheered in by men of HMS *Queen Elizabeth*. (*L. A. K. Boswell, HMS* Queen Elizabeth)

A Belgian machine-gun crew in action against an enemy aircraft. The problem of devising a revolving gun-mounting for anti-aircraft duties has been solved by the simple adaptation of a wagon wheel. The pipe smoker on the left holds a clip of ammunition for the French-built Hotchkiss machine-gun. (*E. Jhek, Belgian Army*)

Left An Englishman, Norman Janes, a sergeant of the London Irish Rifles, (on the left) has exchanged uniforms with a French soldier, the latter characteristically retaining a Gallic stance. The photograph was taken near Vermelles in 1915. (*N. Janes*)

Russians in Salonika with a regimental banner bearing the Csarist Imperial Eagle emphasize the wide range of Allied commitment to the Macedonian Front. (*Miss K. Ussher, Scottish Women's Hospitals*)

A Serbian Cavalry Staff Captain at Mladenovatz Railway Station in September, 1915. (*Miss E. M. Gould, Nurse with 1st British Field Hospital for Serbia*)

An Italian soldier of one of the Bersaglieri regiments in 1918. The distinctive cockerel feathers were retained even when wearing a steel helmet. (*W. Barraclough, 11th West Yorks, in Italy*)

Opposite Repose for an assorted group of French soldiers in a canteen late in 1916, the *poilu* having respect for his wine as the Tommy had for his mug of tea. (*Miss A. E. McClelland, VAD Nurse in France*)

Ensign George L. Compo, a pilot of the United States Naval Air Service, one of several US pilots serving at RNAS, Cattewater, early in 1918. (*J. H. Bentham, RNAS, Cattewater*)

A French Senegalese soldier in Macedonia shares a pool with a Briton in the serviceman's universal chore, his personal laundry duties. (*Sir Thomas Harley, then 9th Battalion King's Own Royal (Lancaster) Regiment*)

Men of the Chinese Labour Corps – here at Fort Renny in Devon with a member of the Corps' own police force standing sentry over an isolation hut. (*A. H. Gitsham, RFC*)

British Medical Officers check for signs of trachoma in this 1918 eye inspection of men from the Chinese Labour Corps in France. (*M. Whiting, RAMC*)

Comradeship in Captivity: A mixed bag of prisoners at Giessen Camp in Germany in 1915. The group includes French soldiers, one a Senegalese wearing his medals, as well as British soldiers in this camp for 'other ranks'. On the original photograph, the German on the left is labelled as "Sank the good guard." (*H. Howland, 7th Battalion, 1st British Columbia Regiment*)

Left Captors and Captives. German troops, including a sailor or marine to the left, escort British prisoners through Bruges. (*G. I. White, RNAS*)

Opposite Some Allied military authorities, in marked contrast to the British, did not seem to frown upon the presence of women in or near their front line positions. Here, in late 1914, a member of the First Aid Nursing Yeomanry, a British unit, is pictured crouched in a Belgian gun emplacement during her visit to the battery position. The gun is actually one of the famous French '75's'. (*Miss Mary D. Marshall, with the First Aid Nursing Yeomanry in Belgium at the time*)

Two women of the First British Field
Hospital for Serbia photographed with
Serbian officers near front line positions at
Pirot in October, 1915. (*Miss E. M. Gould, a
nurse with this Field Hospital*)

Nursing staff at Clonmel in County
Tipperary, the Headquarters of No 12
(Irish) District of the St John Ambulance
Brigade are inspected by Dr Ella Webb. The
inspection takes place at their HQ, the local
borstal. (*Miss A. E. McClelland, British Red
Cross St John Ambulance Brigade*)

British Red Cross Voluntary Aid Detachment driver mechanics attend to the needs of one of their ambulances, a presentation vehicle purchased with money from the Indian province of Sind. The donor of the photograph is kneeling, her colleagues from left to right being the Misses English, Hardy, Dewhurst and Marrable. (*Miss A. E. McClelland*)

Naval construction work at Vickers, Barrow. (*P. H. L. Archives*)

Ruth Agnes Paull, a munitions worker at Messrs Bickford Smiths of Camborne in Cornwall. (*Mrs R. Preston*)

Wearside shipwrights at the Sunderland firm of Shorts. At this early stage of the war they cannot realize what phenomenal endeavour will be required in the yards to cope with the replacement of merchant ships sunk by German U boats. (*Miss B. Scott, munitions worker*)

A wedding in the air. Apparently a service wedding with the happy couple allowed to don civilian clothes for the occasion. The uniformed guests are all RAF or WRAF which dates the picture to 1918 or 1919. The location is an RAF Station in Kent. (*Mrs M. Archdale, WRAF*)

An all-women Concert Party (despite appearances!) entertains children in a park at Lemington on the Tyne in 1917. (*West Newcastle Local Studies Group, Benwell Library, Newcastle upon Tyne*)

A group of German Stormtroopers. The tactical concept of lightly equipped, fast-moving assault troops was not solely German but on the Eastern Front and then in their Spring Offensive in 1918 in the West, the Germans used it to great effect. The men here display their key weapons and equipment, the Mauser rifle, the stick grenade, the wire cutters and, in the hands of their youthful looking unit leader, a Luger pistol. (*F. Cunnington, Notts and Derby Regiment*)

Germans bring in wounded on the Somme during January, 1917. A translation of the original German caption to this photograph says that it was taken during a truce for the purpose of recovering wounded in the Valley of the Ancre. (*L. Kalepky, 86th Regiment of Fusiliers, Königen Regiment*)

Party night in a German airmen's Mess (Flieger Abteilung 240). As in the Royal Flying Corps, the officers were drawn from other branches of the Army as can be seen from the differing styles of collar. The German haircuts are surely shorter but the party spirit would not be out of place on similar occasions in an RFC Mess. (*F. Cunnington*)

A regimental mix of Bulgarian soldiers. The Bulgarians did not merely 'keep occupied' a huge Allied force in Macedonia, their country lost a higher proportion of its male service age population than either Germany or France. This photograph was found by a British soldier in an abandoned dugout in 1918. (*M. MacEwen, RGA*)

PART FIVE

Talisman and Crucifix.

MOST MEN in the line managed to cope with the presence of death and disfigurement. Some of them were by nature phlegmatic, not readily moved to strong emotion, others were tutored by trench education to acceptance of their fate. High explosive shell fragment, shrapnel ball or bullet would leave them unharmed unless fate were to decree otherwise. If the latter were the case, then neither precautions nor prayers would deflect destiny. Such a philosophy was a powerful protective, linked as it was to the further psychological armour subconsciously worn by many – that what had happened to so and so could not happen to oneself. The element of uncertainty, however, the potential of sudden wound or death, the terrifying vulnerability of the priceless treasure of life, such nightmare thoughts fuelled belief in agencies of guardianship. Such agencies cannot easily be classified in that material and spiritual elements are in the same compound. The wistful security engendered by sight and touch of the locket with photograph and tiny ribboned curl of hair, the four-leaf clover, the St Christopher medallion, the pressed flower picked in a familiar meadow, were obviously tangible but, more than this, body and soul were sustained. The more imaginative the man, the more he looked for beneficent meaning in coincidence. By the same token the more he feared evil in nightmare or the more readily he recognized omen. Superstition governed the thoughts of many and rumour exercised influence on most.

It is particularly sad to read the letters of men preoccupied with death when we know that their disturbing premonitions would in fact be realized. Some, perhaps, were merely covering for all eventualities in writing last letters to be read in the event of their death but others would write a series of letters, each darkly shadowed by foreboding.

Not surprisingly some soldiers took refuge in imagined manifestations of divine protection. Angelic hosts holding back Teutonic hordes at Mons were the earliest and best known of the heavenly images 'incontestably' observed. Henry V's Agincourt bowmen were to follow. To be fair, we should recognize that, as well as spiritual sensibilities being hyper-activated by stress, the ground itself was historically hallowed. English Kings of the Middle-Ages, a celebrated Tudor, two of the Lord Protector's Major Generals and two invincible Dukes had each with his men wrought deeds here on which every member of the 20th century Expeditionary Force had been schooled with variable success. It is clear that some men found a sort of mystic communion in this, something which further animated belief in their cause.

A talisman inspiring widespread belief was the 'miraculously' suspended Virgin and Child on the tower of Albert Cathedral. The fact that the huge gilded figure was for long roped to prevent its fall was less well known than the 'certainty' that when it fell the war would end. The failure of the war to end when the statue fell did not retrospectively damage the significance of an image which would be long recalled by those who had difficulty in remembering other details of their time in France.

The extent to which the symbol behind the statue actually upheld the soldier can only be measured in the individual. The war challenged much that had been assumed without question and faith came under the sort of personal scrutiny unthinkable hitherto, except for that tiny number of men inwardly called upon to examine the foundations of their belief. Generalizations are often thought-provoking puddings overflavoured by the cook's preference, but it would generally be agreed that the denominational description stamped on the soldier's identity disc represented a pre-war church or chapel Sunday attendance in far greater numbers than those with which we are familiar today. Perhaps we may go further and suggest that within so many people who practised Sunday Observance there was again a number whose daily life had its time for prayer and was carried out in thought and deed in due conformity to spiritual belief and church teaching. Soldiering could therefore make an impact upon adherence to an institutional framework of religion and also upon the personal faith of the individual. The Army's Sunday Church Parade was unable to offer much encouragement to voluntary adherence to collective worship. Its identification with compulsion by Army authority devalued spiritual meaning, affronted as this was also likely to be by the scarcely disguised disdain of the unbelievers. Furthermore the Padre, representative of the worthwhile nature of the whole exercise, was tested in a way no country or town vicar was ever examined. If he were to fail as a man among men, he damaged far more than himself. He could, in spiritual terms, do the devil's work of subversion. Unsurprisingly, for all the inspirational beacons of numerous Padres, post-war congregations after the thankfulness of victory would be gravely diminished by the absence of those men who had not been convinced that an omnipotent God could have permitted man's free will to create such awful carnage. In any case many had found something more satisfying for a Sunday. It allowed for later rising, and then a stroll to sup ale in masculine conviviality at the Local. Acceptance of the church or chapel's unquestioned rôle in the layman's life was on a downward slope to dismissal.

Of personal faith, the evidence is so strong in individual cases of outright contemptuous rejection and wondrous reaffirmation that the safer ground for widely-based conclusions is that most men needed something upon which to lean and, among the agencies of support, faith indubitably brought comfort to some. For others it was either insufficiently rooted, too frequently challenged or too horrifically confronted to survive. However, so searing was the impact of a material world that, not unlike the image of a leaking reservoir of courage, the will to maintain, in the post-war world, an active positive faith was reduced by the wartime demands upon that faith as well as by imprisonment in a new world unpurged of the evils of the old. It is ironic that it was the unwilling soldier, the conscripted conscientious objector, when such a man was moved by spiritual conviction, who found in his faith such a sure shield against every weapon thrust at him by military or civil authority.

In consideration of the soldier's state of mind and as a chilling negation of the utility of such philosophical contemplation in some cases, we ought perhaps to bear witness to those whose experience had unhinged their minds and hurled them beyond the reach of normal intercourse with their fellows. Some men through sudden shattering experience – commotional shell shock – were to remain for an indefinite period cut off from their fellows. Experimental treatment, including the administering of electric charges, nursed some back to recovery or the fringe of normality but the permanently war-disabled would include men institutionalized for life through injury to the mind. Long-lasting damage, too, was done to some men by prolonged exposure to experiences beyond their capacity to endure and these shell-shock victims added to the numbers of those for whom neither talisman nor crucifix had availed.

Family pride. There is little doubt that Mr &
Mrs Hodgson of Sunderland would keep
this framed photograph in a prominent
place. Their son had enlisted in the local
regiment, the Durham Light Infantry.
(*Mrs Ledger*)

A father and son portrait taken at Wareham
in Dorset on 26 September, 1915. Sergeant
J. S. Canovan of the East Lancashire
Regiment has a son who seems to have
ambitions to serve in a more Northerly based
regiment. (*E. F. G. Chapman, East
Lancashire Regiment*)

Practical aids to learning anatomy are somewhat lugubriously displayed as talismen by men of the 2/1st West Lancashire Field Ambulance of the Royal Army Medical Corps. The recruits pictured here in October, 1914, are still without uniform. (*A. P. Pickthall, RAMC*)

continent of Europe, it is well to be very sure that we can with a clear conscience claim His promised presence with us.

And there are just three considerations I should like briefly to set before you.

I. No one can for a moment doubt that Great Britain was forced into the present war, utterly against her will, by the paramount obligation of fidelity to plighted faith, and the duty of defending weaker nations against violence and wrong. Nay more, it is increasingly plain that had we been content to purchase peace at the expense of honour, the day of reckoning for us would only have been postponed till France and Russia had been crushed, and Germany had been free to turn her vast military resources against ourselves and reduce Great Britain and Ireland to the deplorable condition of unhappy Belgium. Our cause is in very truth a just one, and though the German Emperor's custom of linking the name of God with his own in defence of his present campaign of plunder, makes one almost hesitate to claim thus publicly the Divine countenance, yet we must never forget that the issue of counterfeit coin does not make us unwilling to use the true metal.

Only let us be very sure that our cause is just. And indeed we may claim that merit, when we realise that England has no material advantage to gain out of the carnage and cruelty of war; while we see most clearly what principles prompted those who provoked it. On the one hand we have the ideals of Jesus Christ—justice

and mercy, honour and truth. On the other a cruel and degraded spirit of militarism based openly on the conduct of Attila and his Huns in the fifth century, who was aptly called "the Scourge of God." We are faced first with the repudiation of the value of moral obligations, designated contemptuously as "a scrap of paper." Then we have the burning and destruction of Louvain, with its great library, the wonder of the world. Then we have foul outrages on women and children, villages and homes ruthlessly destroyed, and unarmed men and women cruelly done to death.

And to what are we to trace all this terrible upheaval, in spite of nineteen centuries of Christian teaching? Is it not due to the prior destruction of all Christian ideals; to the gross materialism of German philosophy; and to the ever-growing Rationalism and Atheism of a once Christian nation. Contrast with all this the conduct towards their enemies of our own soldiers and sailors, "gallant gentlemen, who bore no malice and knew no fear."

II. Then you may claim God's presence, my brothers, because you are going out to fight for your King and country at the sacred call of duty.

Nelson's farewell battle cry has not lost its meaning.

The inscription on the lonely grave of another Lawrence in India has its message for each one of you—"Here lies one who tried to do his duty."

You have heard your country's voice, and you could not resist the call.

III. And closely linked with this is

6

the last thought I would set before you. You have a right to look for the Divine presence, because you are carrying out God's great law of vicarious sacrifice.

At the root of the life work of Jesus Christ lies the glorious truth—"The Son of Man came to give His life, a ransom for many."

And the cross of Jesus is the ever-constant reminder of victory out of seeming defeat, and of never-ending life out of a cruel death.

It is when we remember this that a righteous war becomes a sacred and a religious duty.

There is an expression used in the Old Testament, notably in the Books of Jeremiah and Joel, to which I wish to direct your attention. I take just one passage—Joel 3.9. In our authorised version it reads—"Prepare war, wake up the mighty men." But if you look to the marginal reading you will see that the Hebrew word for "prepare" means to "sanctify."

So the command is, that war is to be undertaken as in God's sight and to be carried on under His direction. Special arrangements had been made for the Jewish priests to hold services for the soldiers, as we are doing in this Cathedral to-day, and to exhort them to courage and hopefulness and mercy. "Prepare war" means then "Sanctify war." Pray for God's blessing upon your undertaking. Ask Him for Jesus Christ's sake to pardon all your sins. Say to Him "O God I belong to Thee: O God I give myself to Thee: wash me and make me clean and take not Thy Holy Spirit from me:" and with this prayer often upon your lips God's

7

presence will go with you, and in life or in death His protecting hand will ever be over you.

You are going out as our representatives. You are leaving Ireland shortly for the honour of each man and woman amongst us; for your loved ones: for your homes: for your very existence and ours as free men or free women, and we for our part won't forget you and the dear ones you leave behind you. Constantly here in God's House of Prayer, and from day to day we will commit you to God's care and keeping, Who is as near to you on the battle field as in cathedral, church or chapel.

"On the one hand we have the ideals of Jesus Christ ... on the other a cruel degraded spirit of militarism based upon the conduct of Attila and his Huns." From a Sermon preached on 20 September, 1914, in St Patrick's Cathedral Armagh by Dr J. D. Crozier, Archbishop of Armagh and Primate of All Ireland to members of the Ulster Volunteer Force, 7th Battalion Royal Irish Fusiliers. (*Brigadier T. E. H. Helby, RGA*)

Guerre 1914-1916

81 — ALBERT (Somme) - Le Clocher de N.-D. de Brebières
après plusieurs bombardements par les Allemands.
The steeple of N.-D. Brebières bombarded by the Germans.

G. Lelong, 21, Rue St-Martin, Amiens

Visé Paris n° 87

222. - Fleurbaix
Le Calvaire.

Commercially produced postcards
characteristically emphasising the survival
of religious images amid so much
destruction (*P. H. L. Archives*)

Symbol of success on the waterfront at
Salonika. British and French soldiers
examining the wreckage of the first enemy
aircraft downed over this front in 1916.
(*William Aitchison*)

"No one's number on it" or, as the original
caption calls it: "a narrow squeak" for the
officers of a Border Regiment Company
Mess in a trench dugout at Vimy in May,
1916. The German unexploded shell which
merely broke through the timbering of the
dugout was a 5.9. (*W. Aitchison*)

A rating from HMS *Inflexible* poses in the hole torn in her plating by a Turkish shell on 18 March, 1915, when this battle cruiser, having struck a mine as well as suffering shell damage, was fortunate not to follow the three Allied battleships sunk by mines in the close bombardment of the forts of the Dardanelles. (*Rear Admiral B. Sebastian, then in HMS* Inflexible)

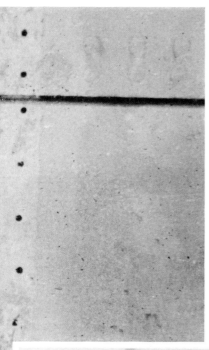

An unkind fate for two donkeys and an escape for their riders. Two Argyll and Sutherland Highlander officers, Captain J. H. Young and Major Eager, on leave and returning from sightseeing in Memphis, were extraordinarily lucky when this palm tree suddenly fell across the necks of their mounts, killing the donkeys but leaving the two officers unharmed. (*Lt-Colonel J. H. Young, Argyll and Sutherland Highlanders*)

Hospitality on the eve of disaster. This poignant photograph was taken at Orphir House in the Orkneys in May, 1916, the month of Jutland. Mrs Winnie Johnston and her family play host to Naval guests from Scapa Flow. She has donned the uniform jacket and cap and carries the telescope of the man whose arm she takes, Rear Admiral Sir Robert Arbuthnot of HMS *Defence*, flagship of the 1st Cruiser Squadron. Two of Sir Robert's officers have also parted with their caps. At 6.20 p.m. on 31 May HMS *Defence* came under concentrated shelling and "disappeared in a roar of flame". There were no survivors from the complement of 903. (*Mrs B. Crosland, the fourth of Mrs Johnston's daughters*)

External recognition and reward. Wilfred Tatham, a Lieutenant in the Coldstream Guards, has proud family accompaniment as he leaves Buckingham Palace following his investiture with the Military Cross by HM King George V. (*W. G. Tatham*)

The end of a leave and the return to France: A troopship about to leave Folkestone harbour, midday 12 March, 1918. The upturned faces of the soldiers on board can be seen as they look up at the airship hovering 100 feet overhead and from which this photograph was taken. The personal fortunes of some of the men on the boat are likely to be determined in less than a fortnight with the German onslaught of 21 March. (*H.R.H. Ward, RNAS, the airship pilot who took this photograph*)

A pet in the Flying Arm. As it happened this ring-tailed lemur, 'Jimmy', in the arms of 2nd Lieutenant Hugh Morkill, a pilot of No 144 Squadron RAF in Palestine in 1918, was occasionally taken up in Morkill's DH9 on flights behind the lines. Jimmy was not taken on the Squadron's work of bombing the retreating Turkish Army between August and October of that year.
(*H. B. Morkill*)

Enemy symbols of inspiration. Among those present at this Imperial visit to Marcke airfield at Courtrai, the home of the most famous aeroplane squadron of the war, Jagdstaffel 11, are Ludendorff (1) Kaiser Wilhelm II (2) Hindenburg (3) and Richthofen (4). Now commanding a fighter wing incorporating his old unit, Manfred von Richthofen can be seen wearing a head bandage, the result of a wound he received in July 1917. He was back in command within a month, long before he was fit. His red-painted Albatros DV stands ready for inspection. (*C. E. Townley, Suffolk Regiment, attached RAF*)

This SE5^A, one of the better fighter planes of the war, has been named "Oonah", probably after a girl friend of the pilot, C. F. Cunningham. The machine is seen at Northolt in October, 1918, serving with 30 Training Depot Station. (*C. S. Wynne-Eyton, RAF*)

British soldiers attached to French units found the presence of a predominantly Catholic regiment's priest very evident. Here a British artilleryman has photographed a French Padre celebrating Mass in trenches near Bailly in July, 1916. (*W. Aitchison*)

Howard Marten, on the left, a Conscientious Objector to Military Service by reason of his Quaker beliefs, had been forcibly enlisted into the Non-Combatant Corps and sent to France where his refusal to obey a military order led to his Court Martial and the pronouncement of a death sentence. It was commuted, after a lengthy pause, to one of ten years' penal servitude. After the commencement of the prison term in England, Marten accepted a new Government Home Office Scheme enabling men in his position to do non-war work under conditions intended to be less harsh than prison. His first spell of such work was in a stone quarry at Dyce near Aberdeen where he is pictured on the occasion of a visit by his mother. The man on the right is also a Concientious Objector who had been sentenced to death, Cornie Barratt. (*H. C. Marten*)

24   12.11.16.

Dear Mother,

Have you heard that
Douglas has been "killed in action"?
It is awful, specially after Dick
having gone too. But we cannot
question the guiding hand of the Lord,
for He knows best and there is a
reason for it all, while they are
far better off with Him than they
ever could be down here.

The same night that I heard from
Dorothy of his death, I was reading
those last verses of I Thess 4
"If we believe that Jesus has died &
risen again, we also believe that
through Jesus God will bring with
Him those who shall have passed
away"

It makes the reason stronger – if
that were possible – why we should
long even more for the Coming of the

"We cannot question the guiding hand of
the Lord". A letter from an Artillery
subaltern whose faith at that time and
thereafter remained undiminished by his
active service in France.
(*Dr M. Webb-Peploe, the subaltern*)

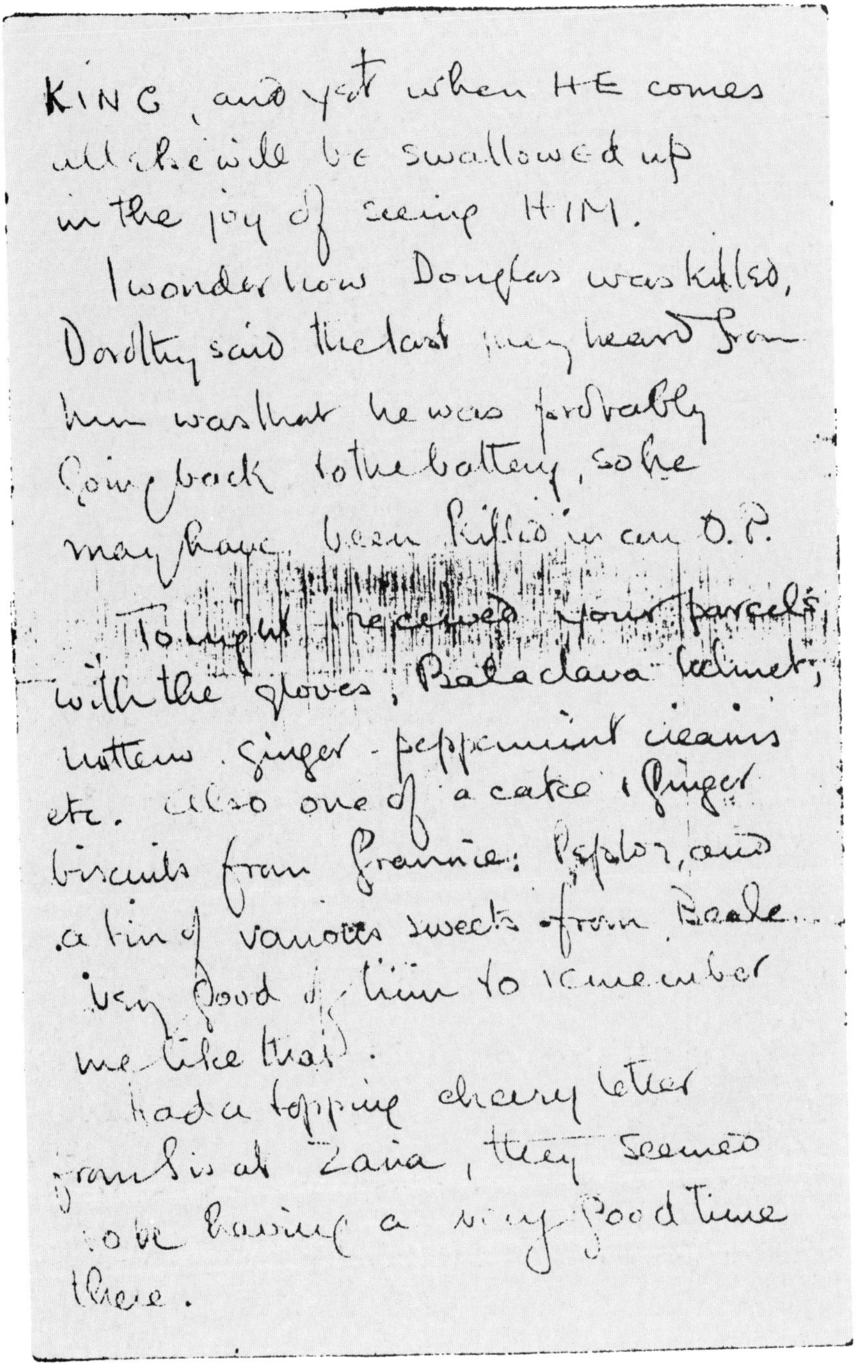

KING, and yet when HE comes
all that will be swallowed up
in the joy of seeing HIM.

I wonder how Douglas was killed.
Dorothy said the last they heard from
him was that he was probably
going back to the battery, so he
may have been killed in an O.P.

Tonight I received your parcels
with the gloves, Balaclava helmet,
mittens, ginger, peppermint creams
etc. also one of a cake, ginger
biscuits from Frannie; Pepsion, and
a tin of various sweets from Beale.
Very good of them to remember
me like that.

Had a topping cheery letter
from Sis at Zara, they seemed
to be having a very good time
there.

3. Had a letter from Hadley, he
must be a few miles North of us
but quite near really, though it
is practically impossible to meet him
I'm afraid. He seems very fit
and is still with Le vick.

Also a priceless letter from
Jacko's small sister Jean, and
one from Alice & Constance
Conway, and one from Mrs Jackson
who also sent me Punch of Nov 1st
So I have them fairly up to date now.

It is often about Jeffar, we
got to know each other so well
at Cambridge, and I do not know
anyone who had so high a sense
of honour or who kept his word so
scrupulously as he did.

... ... my letter of yesterday
all right with the many wants
It strikes me that I must send home
a lot of stuff or take a trunk
full home if I get leave, otherwise
when the spring offensive comes
I shall have to bury half my belongings
. regretfully in a shellhole! I have
accumulated an immense amount of
clothing now ‡. The swiss gouties
would be a great idea, specially as
I am at last returning Schultz's
gumboots!
Our stove is turning out to be a
great success and we can have
hot water for a wash in the morning
and many other things. ~~I~~ I believe
in making things as comfortable as
. possible on active service!
‡ This is only comparatively speaking! ⸰

(right margin, vertical) Compared to infantry possibilities.

5. Well I must censor the men's letters and have a read in bed Today is Sunday – of course there has been more bombardment today than for the last week! It always seems so.

Had a bit of a yarn with an awfully nice Bombadier who looks after the signalling stores. He said he would soon be forgetting the numbers of the hymns! but agreed that the great thing is to know the Lord who is the Same everywhere.

The men here are a ripping crowd on the whole and are settling down to their work well. Had a letter from Godfrey please thank him much.

Much love

Jos. Murray. P.T.O

I finished this off before going out in case I should be some time. I had to go over to another group to find out a code from them. and didn't know how long I should be.

Your letter I got as well as all the others last night, also one from Mrs Jackson. Thank you so much for yours.

Am going to bed now Goodnight.

Opposite "I never called upon God for help". A contemporary account of intense infantry combat closes with a denial of men's thoughts of God in time of danger. (*J. B. Herbert, 2/4 Queens Royal West Surreys*)

33

conscript, not to nothing so vulgar as a Military Service Act, but to the good opinions of my neighbours.

I envy and admire the Conscientious Objector, and I believe his courage to be the true courage. I believe even the splendid, patient doggedness of the men out here is what I call bodily - animal courage, if you will. I am convinced it is outshone by all courage of mind in the eyes of Omniscience, as soul must for ever outshine body.

I might talk of the influence of religious feeling in war, and this at great length, but I will only just say a word or two.

I judge that only an emotional religion of great intensity and Authority could survive any more than any other abstract idea, the chaos of danger. I certainly never saw or heard of any of my men or friends finding time, or remembrance even then, of God.

Personally I held it my one form of true courage, that I never once called upon God for help — that was when a lull came and a space for thought. But even that may be only a personal foible or worn out philosophy.

But the mood I return to the Line in, will be very different to the mood I went up in for the first time. I will remember the sort of reckless excitement of a month ago. — the real romance. It seems romance even now as I review it — the dinner at Brigade mess on the last night behind the Line, the General's weather-beaten

34

rugged face , Evelyn's goodbye in the dark outside , the last glimpse of
the warmth and light : and then the march next day up that
dreary, dreary road ; steel helmets in use at last , the adventure
begun !   And I held it 'adventure' then , indulged in heroics,
thought a thousand silly things , because I didn't know
This time , I know and ' good-bye, adventure ' :
I know, this time I am going to take part in a great Victory , where
last time , I had no dreams of that ; but this time I know too
the racking strain , the wild fear , the dreadful misery of the humble
sharers in Victory.   I know, though , my mood of tomorrow.
I shall not think , or laugh at all , but tramp through the mud
as callously and unconcernedly as them all. It's the old soldier's mood,
and it doesn't take long to learn.   It takes a long time to forget !
   - Poor humanity !   But isn't there an old story of a God
hanged on a cross that men might remember pity and that they
are men ?   But I have seen another "Via Dolorosa" and
a different Cross . I have in my mind the memory of a sentry
on a lonely post of the grim Line , just a weakly boy,
dreadfully tired , wet and chilled through and through , huddled over
a rifle in the eternal rain , & always watching the rustling
grass in front of him and the Very lights starting out of the blackness

35.

Like that other Man. Force and Evil are his persecutors but it is a more subtle torment now. for they call him 'honoured' for his fangs. Will our modern Evil ever remember pity for the men it has crucified and so bring War to an end?

Perhaps, some day but where is now that Master of the Event who shall instantly Shave me Shagpat.

J. Basil Herbert
a/4 Queens.
B.E.F
October 2nd 1918

Les petites françaises n'oublient pas les braves anglais
morts au champ d'honneur
The little french girls Keep green the memory of the brave englishmen
dead on the field of honour

This attractively posed picture postcard conveying a message of unity between France and Britain has special historical interest. Lieutenant Parke of the 2nd Battalion Durham Light Infantry had been killed on 13 October, 1914, near Meteren just South of Ypres in what the Official History of Military Operations records as "the first formal British attack of the War", the capture of a village which, as the postcard shows, was to remain undamaged into the following year. (*P. H. L. Archives*)

Field Dressing Stations were established just behind the lines to administer First Aid to battlefield wounded who may have had their earliest attention from Regimental Aid Posts established in the line or in a captured objective. From the dressing stations the wounded would be sent to Casualty Clearing Stations further to the rear. In this photograph of a dressing station the makeshift arrangements can clearly be seen with both stretcher cases and 'walking wounded' receiving attention, not everyone being distracted by the huge explosion. (*P. H. L. Archives*)

Burial in the field; moments when few of
those present can have remained totally
unmoved by thoughts of their own fate and
of Christianity in War. Here in September,
1916, Major Knight, who had been in
command of a Canadian Machine-Gun
Battery, is being buried. (*G. Scroggie, 1st
Canadian Motor Machine-Gun Brigade*)

Macedonia: Stavros and a war cemetery in
wartime. The two nearest graves are those of
Flight Sub-Lieutenant Valines and
Lieutenant Paynting, killed in a Nieuport
crash in January, 1917. Airmen's graves
were sometimes marked, as here, with
broken propellors made into crosses.
(*T. W. Walker, RNAS*)

30/6/16.

My dear Mother & Father,

This is not an easy letter to write, and I have long refrained from writing it; but now that the Advance seems more than a remote possibility, and is in fact, due to start to-morrow, I had better realise at once that I may not get through it. In fact, I consider it very unlikely that I shall get through it whole. Death has no terrors for me in itself, for (like Cleopatra) "I have immortal longings in me". The prospect of pain naturally appals me somewhat, and I am taking morphia in with me to battle.

We are in Corps Reserve behind Hebuterne, and, should all go well, will not be called upon until the second night and then shall probably be resisting a German counter-attack somewhere near Beaumont-Hamel. But our services may be required at any moment.

I have little to leave except my Love and Gratitude. I should like most of my Shakesperian books to go to Albert. My set of Dickens I should like to be given to Phil. I do not wish Desmond, Ronald or Ruth to be forgotten. I should like to give some of my books to Aunt Flora, (my Dickens Picture Book), Aunt Bona, Dorothea and Jack Berlin. I think that perhaps Uncle M. would like to have some of my Oriental Language books. I should also like Minna to have something — I have had such a happy life compared with her family. I should like to have a special gift sent to Aunt Cecily. To Auntie Reb, Sis, and Uncle Phil, my very, very keen love.

I want my captured flag to go to my Regiment.

I can think of nothing else at present. I have old associations with the North-East Hospital for Children, Bethnal Green and the Great Ormond Street Hospital (where 'Johnny Harmon' died), and should like to give something to each.

For the rest — "If 'tis not now, 'twill be to come". Our cause is a good one and I believe I am doing right in fighting,

To you - Mother and Father - I owe all.   The thought of you two -
and of my brothers - will inspire me to the end.   I often wish
Albert was with me and miss him dreadfully.

        Good-bye!

    "If we shall meet again, why then we'll smile
    If not, why then this parting was well made".

                                (Julius Caesar).

                     יְיָ לִי וְלֹא אִירָא

[i.e. the Lord is on my side, I will not fear what man can do unto me]

                    Your loving son,

                    ERNEST.

I will ask Mr. Ramsay (our Chaplain) to send you this if I fall.

'Death has no terrors for me'. On the eve of
the Battle of the Somme, a subaltern in the
4th Battalion Gloucester Regiment writes a
letter to be posted in the event of his death.
The writer, Ernest Polack, who had some
time earlier distinguished himself in
capturing a German flag planted in
No-Man's-Land, was killed in the attack.
Ernest's brother, Benjamin, was killed in
Mesopotamia leaving his other brother,
Albert, in the Royal Engineers, to survive
the war.
(*A. Polack, RE*)

Overleaf A Military Cemetery in Le Tréport
is the scene for the Military Funeral of a
VAD nurse in 1916, a funeral which is
attracting many local people. One of the
vehicles from the Le Tréport British Red
Cross VAD Ambulance Convoy is being
used as the hearse. (*Miss A. E. McClelland,
Le Tréport VAD Ambulance Convoy*)

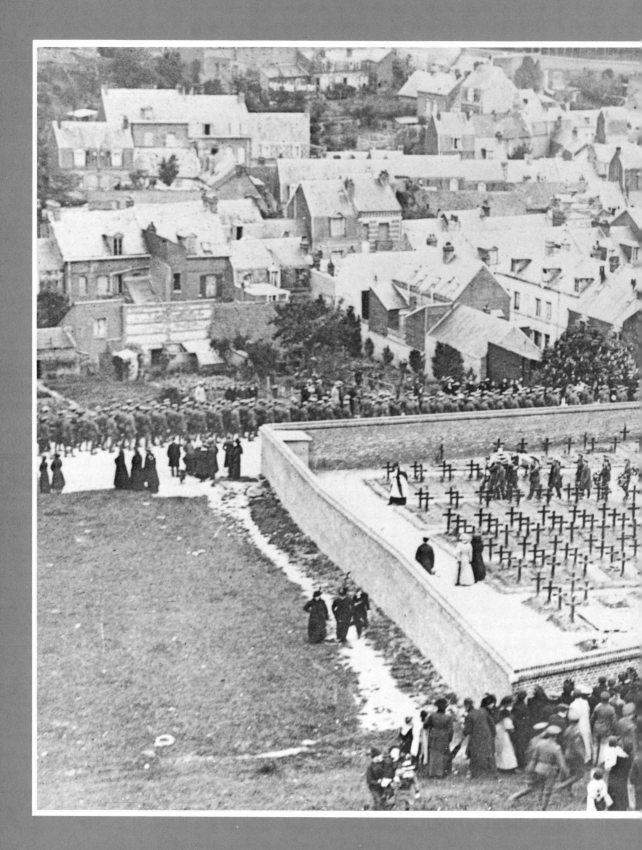

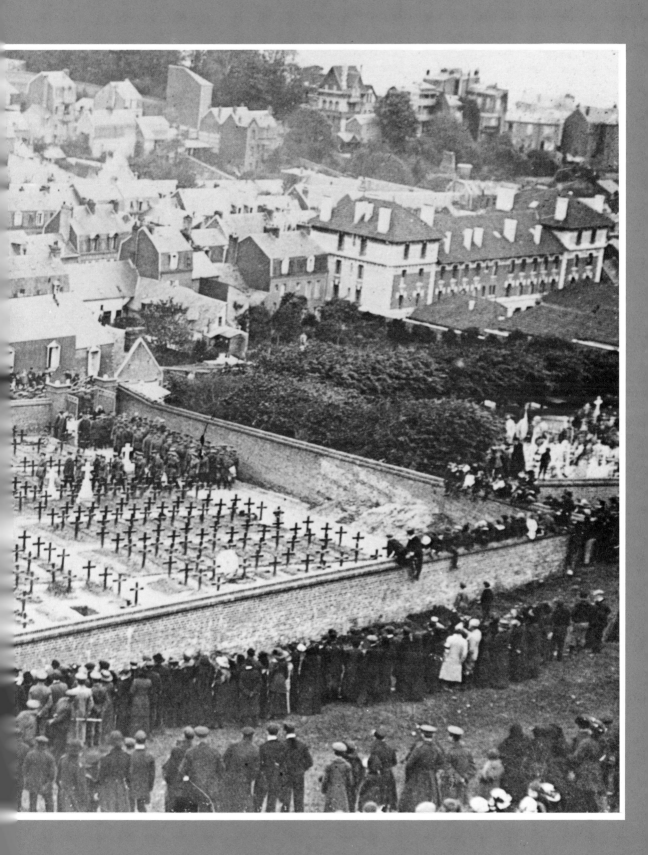

A burial location registration sheet kept by a Padre serving with the 74th Infantry Brigade in the Ypres Salient during the 3rd Battle of Ypres, the opening infantry assault of which was on 31 July, 1917. (*Canon M. S. Evers, the Padre*)

Opposite Neither talisman nor crucifix availed this poor man, nor has decent burial dignified his remains. Shelling at Vimy in 1916 has exposed grim evidence of a former French tenant of this part of the line now being held by the British. Circumstances may have required a hurried burial at the time of the man's death or he may have been killed and buried by the explosion of a shell or mine. (*J. E. Hibbert, South Lancashire Regiment*)

PART SIX

Climax and Aftermath.

MANY PERSONAL accounts testify to the fact that the individual feelings of servicemen on 11 November, 1918, did not match the picture we may imagine of universally joyful celebration. On the fighting fronts there were official celebrations but it was a time for sobering reflections upon the past and anxious questioning of the future. Sailors certainly soon had the awe-inspiring sight of the grey columns of ships of the German High Seas Fleet coming into the Firth of Forth for surrender, then into Scapa Flow for internment, but even this is recorded with solemn sobriety rather than jubilation. There had been no glorious victory in the sort of battle which had been anticipated and in any case the symbol of victory manifest in the internment was sullied when the Germans scuttled their ships in June, 1919. British soldiers playing a part in the hard-fought advance on the Western Front in the last weeks of war, effecting a series of crossings over strongly fortified obstacles, were conscious of the achievement of victories, not so much of the imminent end of the war. It was this very preoccupation with the successful business in hand which contributed to the sense of anti-climax when abruptly it was all over. Intermixed with a sense of relief, a feeling of awe, a measure of pride and for some, the excitement of being drawn involuntarily into the celebrations of newly liberated towns, were other emotions occasioned by looking back, then looking forwards into an uncertain future. Suddenly for those serving for the duration only, there seemed no purpose in being a soldier but the instant reaction to anticipated demobilization involved consideration of the civilian world. For many men the old certainties were no longer surely founded. There might be no job to which to return, a factor which could breed resentment at its disappearance, change of nature or new occupant, perhaps a woman, – or it could mean that the old job

Opposite The evidence of victory – German prisoners in unprecedented numbers – over 13,000 on 8 August, 1918. (*C. E. Townley*)

held attraction no longer. Change was the element which disturbed all contemplation. The home town had changed, the soldier awaiting demobilization had changed. Where could one find the old or a new niche?

The dark side to the altogether more wholesale celebration which attended the Domestic Front's greeting of the Armistice was the face of those in bereavement awaiting no returning hero. In flag bedecked villages or wildly joyful cities, submerged but present, were many widows, orphans or prospective spinsters whose future was in its way as uncertain as those of many of the men waiting to divest themselves of khaki. Unclear too was the future of those who had seen the Services as a professional calling. Among the most obvious of the consequences of peace would be the drastic reduction of the armed forces. There was no need for such strength and an economy undergoing transformation for peace could ill afford the expense of maintaining much capacity for war. It would not be long before an economic axe would sharply sever the career prospects of Naval, Air and Army officers and men, throwing them upon a flooded labour market.

A major part of the social transformation was of course the demobilization itself. It was an Herculean problem beside which cleaning the Augean stables would have been a weekend allocation. A number approaching five million had to be demobilized and integrated into a society and an economy radically altered by the demands of war and now requiring as radical a change. The number may defy imagination but consideration of the well-nigh impossible nature of the task in a democratic society must be made in order to see the true origin of the disillusionment which stained society in the interwar years. The lack of employment opportunity was a source of bitter discontent to the returning serviceman. Dreadful housing conditions often deepened his resentment. The popular slogan "Homes fit for heroes to live in' soon took on a mantle of discredit. Houses could not be turned out to meet the demand and pre-war working-class housing provision was sadly substandard. What remains vividly in the mind's eye of the author as an image more clearly exemplifying disillusionment than anything else is the ex-soldier who had served well on the Gallipoli Peninsula and in France reduced to looking for bottles on a County Durham beach to collect the deposits due on their return. The very demobilization process could be long enough to fuel trouble, as indeed it did in several serious instances, most notably at Calais and in North Wales. The tedious prolongation of Army routine into what must have seemed pointless weeks of frustration was inevitably provocative. Army education courses, however thoughtfully conceived or efficiently run, were a restraint upon the citizen soldier who now saw himself simply as a citizen. Leave as such could aggravate the discipline problem because it required a return from the civilian world to that of Army regulations.

For those who crossed into Germany with the Army of Occupation there was some satisfaction and some novel interest too. Continued active service was to offer opportunities for some, but for others, constrained or tempted into ventures little understood and exposed to presentation of opposing political argument such as those occasioned by intervention in Russia, further service tribulations aggravated a sense of being distant from home in a war prolonged unjustifiably beyond its end. In every sense such service was likely to cause as many problems as it had tackled.

At home, society was further disfigured by the spectre of male disablement in every gathering. Disablement was classless but to be unemployed and disabled was a grim legacy of service to one's country and the factors which undermined the protective capacity of the war pension left their own scars.

For women, post-war prospects presented a more complex picture. We may have a proper awareness of the far wider social horizons for women precipitated as a result of the 1914–18 war years but nothing should diminish an awareness too of the anxiety through which many women had lived these years. Among the thousands of women who lost a loved one – and the total of war dead has most recently been assessed at approximately 723,000 – there were those for whom the lamp of their life had quite literally been put out. As one woman of humble background wrote so movingly to a Padre, "I have had so much trouble in my life having no parents, and my husband and his love was the world to me and I feel as though I want God to take me also." Respect for the War Widow was scant compensation for this woman or for those like her denied the opportunity of partnership in a home or raising a family.

Not infrequently there had been weeks of uncertainty when a man was posted as missing, some women bearing the burden of fruitless hope into the 1920's that a missing husband's homecoming would be granted by the return of his lost memory. The toll of the Nation's manhood also heavily circumscribed the marriage prospects of young women. The 1920's phenomenon of the spinster school teacher or nurse devoted to her charges has a sad relationship to the war. This sombre picture, totally true in its general nature and detail, must not be left unrelieved by lighter colours. With husbands at the War, women were drawn into the making of family and personal decisions, and so gained in authority and experience. For single girls there was a new freedom too, a discarding of some of the Victorian notions of parental control. New thresholds were crossed, social frontiers of exclusion were breached. Substitute or war-generated labour in munitions works, heavy engineering, shipyards, forestry and farming fulfilled more than simply the nation's requirements and where women marched into clerical and secretarial work they were going to capture and hold employment territory. They were to come up against disparagement and discrimination, but such injustice, if not actually put to flight, was often discredited by the performance of women in their work and this would include their increased entry into the professions.

On every hand there was evidence of the indispensability of the woman in the War effort. There could be no retreat from such a re-appraisal of their social standing. The 1918 granting of the vote, albeit grudgingly and limited to women over thirty, did but symbolize a new outlook for women and upon women. The conventions which kept 'decent' women out of pubs, limited the acceptability of the female smoker and shrouded in social disapproval the wider knowledge of birth control were further symbols to be jettisoned in the new spirit of independence and adventure.

The war, for all its awfulness, had also introduced men to adventure, and a new sort of freedom. Escaping from unemployment, unpleasant or monotonous jobs, parental restrictions or family responsibilities and all for what could undeniably be claimed as an unselfish cause, led many men to regard their war service as a very precious experience, something to be cherished and when possible to be reanimated. In a fine book, *The Myriad Faces of War*, Professor Trevor Wilson cautions us against looking back regretfully to good old days. He relates such an attitude to the drying up at an early date of most people's capacity to feel things deeply. It is a sharp point, but I doubt whether it penetrates to the heart of the veteran First World War soldier's kinship with his youthful experience. Indeed, some men would make more of their war-time service than merely the significance to them of comforting memories of comradeship. One such has written that his experience had been his yardstick and reference point for all manner of judgements in his later life in varied employment: "Especially at moments of real problem and confusion – the knack of quick selection of the right priority, the trained ability to sort things out in one's stride." He, as a one-time subaltern, had "often to act on the spur of the moment, yet be sure we chose the right direction. There was no personal credit in all this – it just became instilled I think

from sheer necessity of joint survival under fire." Another man has written that, "I had such friends then as I had never had before or since – friends with whom one lived in a complete bond of thoughts as well as goods. When peace came, the bond was destroyed. We drifted back to the alien ways of our different social levels, our different environments and careers. Perhaps, most significantly, we lost our masculine exclusiveness."

The glory of victory, too, was soon lost and was to seem but a hollow prize. Beneath the shallow satisfaction of triumphal parades, occupying forces and the imposition of peace terms, lay the age-old antipathies still exciting apprehension. Of course one could be sustained in the knowledge that there would never be another great conflict – the late war had settled that – but the present for many was bleak and the future without much prospect. It was only when looking back at the comradeship, humour and purposeful unity experienced in wartime that some felt any solace. In the least romanticised framework, for the men in the ranks it had been a time without problems of decision-making. You simply did what you were told to do, put up with what everyone else put up with and you got your due – pay, uniform and food – and you got a bonus – fellowship. At the dedication of memorials, with however much sadness, on battlefield pilgrimages, in Old Comrades' Re-unions, such feelings of fellowship were shared and fostered. What had to be done had been done. The Germans had been put down and hope for the future had to be invested in the young. They were not to know that their young would be ready just in time, as men and women, to face the ordeal of war again, a generation later and with the same foe. Such knowledge in the mind of the man on the beach would have been a cruel additional burden.

On the move and in the right direction. Horse-drawn Army Service Corps supply wagons file past soldiers halted at the roadside resting before they themselves must move up towards an advancing battlefront. (*A. H. Kynaston, RFA*)

Overleaf Liberation and short-term new tenants. A Belgian farming family at Lessines welcomes the 2/4 Royal West Surreys in place of the Germans who have just vacated these long-held billets in occupied territory. It is not just the flag and the notice which tell a story here but also the wound and the service stripes on the soldiers seated in front. (*S. W. Vinter, 2/4 Royal West Surreys*)

The band of the 18th Battalion Australian Imperial Force plays the National Anthem at the official announcement by the Battalion's Commanding Officer, Colonel G. F. Murphy, of the signing of the Armistice. Vignacourt, France 11 a.m., 11.11.18. (*J. H. McGregor, 18th Battalion, AIF*)

Australian soldiers and French civilians
gather in the Military Cemetery at
Vignacourt for an Armistice Day address.
(*J. H. McGregor*)

Peace Celebrations over the Tigris at
Baghdad – a time-exposure photograph.
(*R. C. Morton, 2/6 Sussex Regiment*)

In this post-Armistice photograph, the Army Service Corps personnel shown with a lorry-drawn 6″ howitzer may be at peace with the Germans but not with the British Army demobilization authorities. A placard enquires: "When will the 1914 and 1915 men go home?" Nevertheless the howitzer is credited on a smaller sign with having fired 11,004 shells and is "Good for a few more on the Rhine". (*S. Walker, RGA*)

Armistice Day at No 3 Fighting School, RAF, Sedgeford, seems to provide as much to ponder over as to celebrate. (*F. C. Ransley, RAF*)

20 November, 1918, the day before the German High Seas Fleet was to be received into British internment, His Majesty King George V on board the American Battleship *New York* is photographed with, from left to right, the Commander-in-Chief Grand Fleet, Admiral Sir David Beatty, the American Admirals Rodman and Sims and the Prince of Wales. This was the first occasion on which a British Sovereign had inspected a ship of the United States Navy. (*L. A. K. Boswell of HMS* Queen Elizabeth)

An aerial photograph which captures both the symbol and the fact of German naval surrender. As required by the Royal Navy, a German U boat, entering Harwich for internment, flies the White Ensign above the flag of the German Imperial Navy. (*L. E. Shelley, RAF*)

Left Students in Cambridge celebrate the Armistice. Some will engage upon a diversion from this patriotic 'motorcade' in order to ransack a nearby centre of Pacifist activity, Bertrand Russell's premises in Trinity Street. (*Hilda Sebastian, then as Hilda Gosling a Girton College student*)

The war is over but the symbolic significance of this British unit crossing into German territory in late November, 1918, is not lost on the men marching with fixed bayonets to the music of their band. (*H. R. Skerritt, RAF*)

Armistice Day at the Army Hospital, Netley, near Southampton, finds some of the convalescents demonstrating their fitness. The Nursing Staff don't seem to disapprove but for two or more Anzacs on the roof, home must seem further away than it ought to be at such a time. (*T. E. Hulbert, 3rd Skinner's Horse*)

Ruling the streets of Cologne as well as the waves, a Royal Naval Contingent, part of the British Army of Occupation, parades the White Ensign through the German city. The four men escorting the flag bearer are Royal Marines, behind them are Royal Naval ratings. (*R. W. James, RN*)

It is probably just after the cessation of hostilities and Miss Audrey Charlesworth, an ambulance driver of the First Aid Nursing Yeomanry, has been offered a joy ride by Major Eustace Ainslie, RAF. The aircraft, with its engines warming up, is a DH10 Amiens, a twin-engined bomber which, with but one exception, arrived on the Western Front too late to see action. (*Miss Mary D. Marshall, First Aid Nursing Yeomanry*)

Opposite Street party for children of Edward Street, Blaydon in County Durham to celebrate the end of the war. (*J. R. Neale*)

Though the war is over, VAD driver
mechanics are among those who have to
return to France for continuing duties. The
party here is disembarking at Boulogne.
(*Miss G. Milburn, VAD*)

New fields for glory. Sportswomen and men
meet His Majesty King George V at the
opening of the Civil Service Sports
Grounds at Chiswick. The King spent some
time watching, among other matches, one
between the Civil Service Women's XI and a
team of the Women's Royal Naval Service.
When it was pointed out to him that the
'Wrens' existed now only as a hockey team,
the King was reported to have "laughed
heartily". The Captain of the 'Wren' Team,
the donor of this photograph, scrutinises the
King from the left hand side of the man in
the white shirt. (*Miss E. Gledstanes*)

One man's price. Lieutenant S. A. J. Levey, 11th Battalion Prince of Wales's Own West Yorkshire Regiment suffered his injuries at Hill 60 during the Battle of Messines which opened on 7 June, 1917. Here he is on convalescence at Fowey in Cornwall. In peacetime Levey was a professional songwriter. (*J. D. Todd, 11th Battalion, West Yorkshire Regiment*)

Trafalgar Day in London in 1919 commemorating both Trafalgar and the Naval victory of the late war. (*Admiral Sir T. H. Binney*)

National Federation of Discharged & Demobilised Sailors & Soldiers,
POPLAR No. 1 BRANCH—48, Ida Street.

Proceeds in aid of FATHERLESS CHILDREN'S FUND (Summer Outing)

A DANCE

— To be held at —

POPLAR TOWN HALL,
THURSDAY, APRIL 10th, 1919,

Commencing at 7 p.m.

Doors open at 6.30 p.m.

M.C. - Mr. A. BOOKER.

Catering at Popular Prices.

Up-to-Date Band in attendance.

Tickets 1/6 each.

RUSSELL BELLMAN, Hon. Sec.

`223

A fund-raising dance for a summer outing
in 1919. The charitable work done
nationally for war orphans is shown locally
here in London by the Poplar Branch of the
National Federation of Discharged and
Demobilised Sailors and Soldiers.
(R. Bellman)

An unusual concourse of vehicles at
Kempton Park racecourse and its environs
in May, 1919. The Ministry of Munitions
parked here for disposal by auction to
interested parties, over 6,000 cars, vans and
lorries which were now surplus to service
requirements. (*Sir Claude V. Holbrooke,
ASC*)

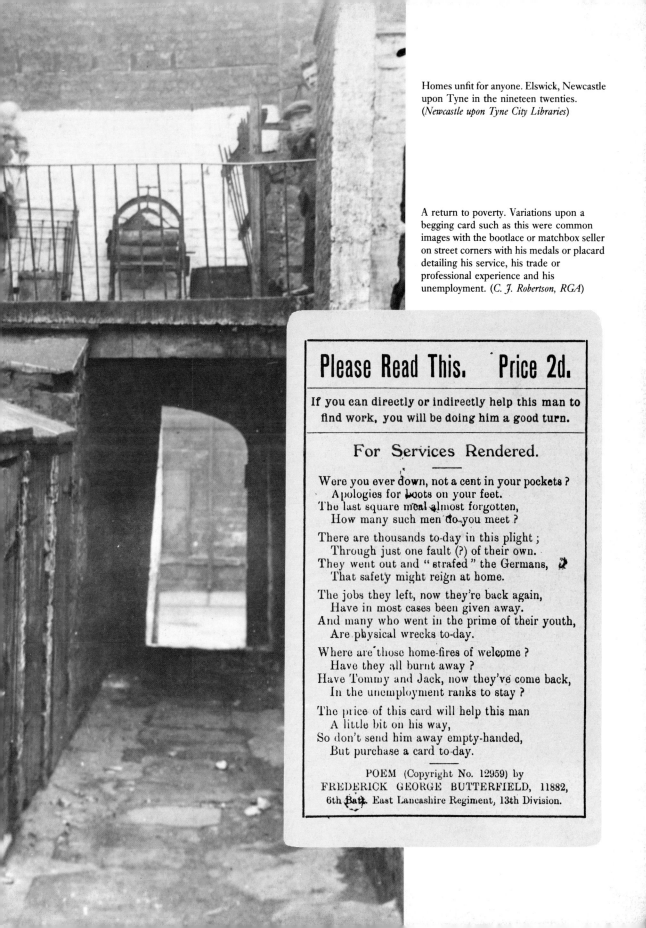

Homes unfit for anyone. Elswick, Newcastle upon Tyne in the nineteen twenties. (*Newcastle upon Tyne City Libraries*)

A return to poverty. Variations upon a begging card such as this were common images with the bootlace or matchbox seller on street corners with his medals or placard detailing his service, his trade or professional experience and his unemployment. (*C. J. Robertson, RGA*)

Please Read This.   Price 2d.

If you can directly or indirectly help this man to find work, you will be doing him a good turn.

For Services Rendered.

Were you ever down, not a cent in your pockets?
    Apologies for boots on your feet.
The last square meal almost forgotten,
    How many such men do you meet?

There are thousands to-day in this plight;
    Through just one fault (?) of their own.
They went out and "strafed" the Germans,
    That safety might reign at home.

The jobs they left, now they're back again,
    Have in most cases been given away.
And many who went in the prime of their youth,
    Are physical wrecks to-day.

Where are those home-fires of welcome?
    Have they all burnt away?
Have Tommy and Jack, now they've come back,
    In the unemployment ranks to stay?

The price of this card will help this man
    A little bit on his way,
So don't send him away empty-handed,
    But purchase a card to-day.

POEM (Copyright No. 12959) by
FREDERICK GEORGE BUTTERFIELD, 11882,
6th Batt. East Lancashire Regiment, 13th Division.

At Murmansk in North Russia in the Winter
of 1918–19, officers and ratings of Royal
Naval vessels based in this most northerly
port were brought into contact with what was
for them an unfamiliar form of supply
transport – reindeer-drawn sledges.
(*W. Williams, RN*)

Major-General Sir Edmund Ironside, in
command of the Expeditionary Force to
North Russia, arrives on board the aircraft
carrier HMS *Pegasus* at Archangel in
October, 1918. Ironside's personal transport
can be seen in the background in the form of
a Fairey Seaplane. (*W. A. Spranklin, RAF*)

British tanks unloaded from SS *Frienfels* at
Novorossisk on the Eastern Shores of the
Black Sea await rail transportation on
2.11.19 to a Tank School at Taganrog. The
tanks, part of a huge amount of war materiél
sent to Russia, were part of a great Allied
endeavour which would be (despite the
basket in the foreground) no postwar picnic.
The support was to prove of no avail and, for
whatever reasons intervention were to have
been launched, it was to be for no fruitful
end. (*General Sir Evelyn Barker, Kings Royal
Rifles, at this time Staff Officer with Mission of
Lt-General Sir C. J. Briggs*)

Opposite The years immediately following
the war saw all over the world the erection
and dedication of commemorative
memorials. Every village had its sons lost to
the Great War. Among the unit memorials
of particular interest was that to the Imperial
Camel Corps, unveiled in the Embankment
Gardens, London in 1921 by Sir Philip
Chetwode, the Commander of the 20th
Army Corps in Palestine and Syria in
1917–18. The tall figure to the left of the
monument is Lord Winterton, a former
Major in the Camel Corps. (*L. Moore,
Imperial Camel Corps*)

Drawn back by an indestructible bond. No
longer in uniform, men, once of the Royal
Naval Division, revisit the Somme area in
1924. They were to journey to Gallipoli and
to return again and again to the Western
Front, witnesses of the flowering of some
seeds in the barren wasteland of war.
(*E. F. Wettern, RND*)

SUGGESTED FURTHER READING

A new stimulating history of Britain in the Great War is that of Trevor Wilson *The Myriad Faces of War* (Polity Press, Cambridge 1986). The nature of the war in its 20th industrial and technological context is convincingly explained in John Terraine's *White Heat, The New Warfare 1914–18* (Sidgwick and Jackson, London 1982) while that of soldiering on the Western Front is clearly examined by John Ellis in *Eye Deep In Hell*, Croom Helm, London, 1976.

The family link from soldier to civilian in nicely caught in *Grandfather's Adventures in the Great War 1914–1918* by Cecil M. Slack (Stockwell, Ilfracombe 1977). The experience of women is looked at in *Women at War 1914–1918* by Arthur Marwick (Fontana, London, 1977) while E. S. Turner in *Dear Old Blighty* (Michael Joseph, London 1980) pictures a wider Domestic Front canvas. Peggy Hamilton's memoir *Three Years or the Duration* (Peter Owen, London 1978) is outstanding on munitions factory work while *Auntie Mabel's War*, compiled by Marian Wenzel and John Cornish (Allen Lane, London 1980), *The Quality of Mercy* by Monica Krippner (David and Charles, Newton Abbot 1980) and *Elsie Fenwick in Flanders* (Spiegl Press, Stamford 1980) all have great appeal.

Of soldiering memoirs, a gunner writes well in P. J. Campbell's *The Ebb and Flow of Battle* (Hamish Hamilton, London 1977), a sapper does the same in John Glubb's *Into Battle* (Cassell London 1978) and an infantryman likewise in H. E. L. Mellersh's *Schoolboy into War* (William Kimber, London 1988). There is much of interest in Jon Cooksey's book on the Barnsley Pals published by the Barnsley Chronicle and the newly published diaries of Lord Moyne, *Staff Officer* edited by Brian Bond (Leo Cooper 1987) may well become a classic of its kind.

For anyone interested in the serviceman as such on active service, then he may find interest in my trilogy *The Sailor's War 1914–1918* (Blandford Press, Poole 1985), *The Airmen's War 1914–1918* (Blandford Press, Poole, 1987), or *The Soldier's War 1914–1918* (Arms and Armour, London, 1988).

*Photograph on back endpapers
by courtesy of John Garfield.*

Peter Liddle